Wedding Showers
for Couples

by
Pamela Thomas

Bridal Guide, Ltd.
P.O. Box 2091
La Crosse, WI 54602

September 1999

Wedding Showers for Couples

First printing   March 1997   First edition   April 1997
Second printing September 1999   Second edition   September 1999

Library of Congress Catalogue Number 99-094668

ISBN: 0-9615882-6-8
SAN: 697-0729
SAN: 697-0737

Printed in the United States of America
SAN 697-0729
SAN 697-0737

Acknowledgments

The following people contributed greatly to the quality, accuracy of content, marketing, design and support. Thank-You.

Saint Mary's Press
Printing
Winona, MN
(507) 457-7900

The Studio Photography
Photos
La Crosse, WI 59601
(608) 782-1080

Gathering Waters Design
Cover Design/Typography
La Crosse, WI
(608) 796-2376

Bruce Thiebauth
Bridal Fair, Inc.
Omaha, NE
(402) 592-8200

Joyce Scardina Becker, CMP
Events of Distinction
San Francisco, CA
(415) 751-0211

Lisa Kratt
Recipes
La Crosse, WI

Dedicated to
my family with love.

Richard G. Williams, my husband, my strength,
my friend, my love.

Betty Thomas, my loving mother

Especially to my father, Dale, and my sister, Kim,
who can no longer be here to share my love for
them. You are both very missed
by us all.

My precious niece, Brittany West and nephews
Nicholas and Christopher West

My special friends, Kay Robinson,
Ingrid Radke, Jeff Moen and Dale, Lois Moen,
Kris & Nick Harring, Claudia Schwaegerl, Patty Niedbalski,
Sharon Fogel and Denny, Kim and Tom Lewandowski, "Mushy",
Tina Mashak, Roxanne and Pierre Santéle,
Butch & Lola Monsoor, Ann Allen,
Robert Michaels,
Kathy & Gary Arentz
and Mary Messer

In memory of

Thelma & Victor Clark and Earl "Pete" Thomas
my grandparents,
Kathy Brindley and Rick Erickson

About the Author

A graduate in journalism from Marquette University, Pamela Thomas-Williams has been employed as a copywriter for a variety of advertising agencies, including her own. A winner of several advertising awards, she teamed up with numerous consultants to devise the best guide to shower planning. Pamela is also the author of the best selling *BRIDAL GUIDE, THE COMPLETE GUIDE TO PLANNING YOUR WEDDING,* now in its 6th edition with over 100,000 copies sold. This includes a Spanish version of this book entitled *GUÍA NUPCIAL.*

Listed in Who's Who of American Women in 1988 and Who's Who of the Midwest 1997, she is also active in Sigma Delta Chi, PRSA, as well as numerous bridal related associations. Pamela continues her writing and speaking efforts on the topic of weddings with such companies as Bridal Fair, Inc. and Carlson Craft wedding invitations.

Disclaimer

Wedding Showers for Couples is designed to be a thorough, step–by–step handbook for brides and their families to use while planning a wedding shower. It would be impossible to reprint all the information that is potentially available to the author/publisher, as there are many other resource books that deal with specific needs and types of weddings.

Every effort has been made to make this handbook as complete and as accurate as possible. It is with the assistance of many professionals that this book has been as comprehensive as it is. However, be aware that changes are frequently made and errors are possible.

Hopefully, this book will serve you well as a guide, and you will find it both informative and interesting to read. The author and publisher shall have neither liability nor responsibility to any person or entity with respect to any loss or damage caused, or alleged to be caused, directly or indirectly, by the information contained within this book.

Introduction

This book was written after 10 years of research in wedding planning and the success of my book entitled ***BRIDAL GUIDE, A COMPLETE GUIDE ON HOW TO PLAN YOUR WEDDING.*** I also came to the conclusion that wedding showers had become stale and boring.

The problem was not showers in themselves. Showers are a tradition and will be a part of weddings forever. The problem was me and millions of others like myself. The lifestyle trends have changed, the way we deal with relationships has changed, and even the way we look at the rituals surrounding the wedding is viewed in an entirely different way.

Love and romance are probably more important than ever before. Couples today, however, are working much harder together to plan their future. They are feeling a deeper sense of need to share almost everything they do as a couple. It is a society that no longer requires a defined line between what women should do and what men should do. The couples getting married today are friends. They have individual careers. They bring with them their own sense of identity. They share financial and domestic responsibilities. They are more open-minded about what it takes to make a marriage work, thus developing patience and understanding for each other's needs.

In taking all of this into consideration, I felt the time had come to write another book that allows this generation to utilize their creativity and serve a newer , more realistic purpose for the traditions. The traditions that they will be responsible for and, perhaps, hand down to their children. It is the memories they will pass on into the new millennium.

I hope you enjoy my book. I am always open to suggestions and ideas. Feel free to write or call. Have a terrific life together, and have fun planning the wedding and showers.

Good luck.

Pamela Thomas-Williams
P.O. Box 2091 LaCrosse, WI 54602-2091
(608) 785-1235

Table of Contents

Chapter 1

A BRIDAL SHOWER

The custom of a "bridal shower" came about when a poor Dutch miller fell in love with a maiden whose father forbade the match and refused to provide a dowry. Some say it was because the Dutch Miller had given all his worldly possessions away to the poor–thus having nothing to give. The miller's friends came to the rescue and "showered" the bride–to–be with enough gifts in order to start housekeeping.

The wedding shower, traditionally a get–together for women only, is now just as likely to include the female and male. A "his and her" shower is a perfect way for the bride's friends and the groom's friends to meet each other. It also is easier to plan showers around what both the bride and groom enjoy. Keep in mind that there is no reason why a close friend or usher cannot give a shower for just the groom.

Today, most men and women are getting married at an older age. Many of them also have individual careers with each of them working full–time. They may have their own respective friends or many other couples that they socialize with. It becomes a great opportunity to meet all of these "new" people. This also means that each may have a lot of everyday household goods, but perhaps lack in a variety of other useful items. I believe that it is not only a good idea, but definitely a lot more fun to share in all of the various wedding activities together. There is the simple fact that there are many retailers who provide bridal registries for the bride AND the groom–to–be. More of that information is covered later on into this book, including a variety of ideas and themes to plan around the bride and/or groom's gift needs and social interests.

Although our social trends have continued to change over the years, you must be aware of the type of wedding, the local customs, and the tastes and circumstances of the bride and groom. There are many couples/families who still prefer the very traditional style of weddings and showers. But regardless of the type of shower that is given, keep in mind that a shower is a party, so it is intended to be fun.

Who Should Host the Shower?

The MOST important point to remember here is that IMMEDIATE FAMILY MEMBERS should NOT give a shower. That includes a mother or sister or future mother–in–law of the bride. The simple reason for that is that it just isn't in good taste to ask for a gift from an immediate member of your family. They may, however, share their home or facility, provide monetary assistance, or assist in organizing the shower, as long as they are not "hosting" the shower. The invitation usually states who is the host(s). Keep in mind that there are many costs that the family and bridal party must incur and you must try to be considerate of that.

It is often a good idea for two or three people to jointly host a shower rather than have too many showers, which can minimize the expenses, as well as some of the responsibility. There are decorations, invitations, food and beverages, hostess gift, and prizes that need to be purchased. The sharing of responsibility is helpful in planning, food preparation, sending out the invitations, and even putting a guest list together. This may enhance the opportunity of having more than one shower – such as one hosted by coworkers–workers, one by neighbors, one by just close friends, etc. Again, location of the shower, the kind of food, decorations, and gifts, including where the bride and groom may have registered for their gifts, may solely depend upon the type of shower you are giving.

Registering for gifts is VERY IMPORTANT. You must stress this to the bride and groom. Even though there are many people and cultures that prefer to give money, there are equally as many traditional people who are uncomfortable with that. They might feel that a special type of gift or a gift that they know you want or need will give you many years of memories of the gift giver. I know this to be true. Secondly, in this day and age, who needs to receive a lot of duplicated gifts? With many couples marrying at an older age, this means that they have also set up individual households already and just don't need many of the traditional, basic items. Thirdly, with the idea of the theme showers there is a tremendous opportunity to receive gifts that truly meet the needs of the bride and groom as a couple, not to mention the needs of the 21st century.

Origin of the Engagement and Wedding Rings

The ring as a symbol of marriage may have evolved from an African custom where the bride and groom's wrists were tied together with grass during the ceremony. And when grooms negotiated purchase of their brides, they often gave metal rings as partial payment. Eventually, the more precious the metal the wealthier the groom. In ancient Egypt before coins were minted, gold rings were used as currency. To show he trusted his wife with his money, the Egyptian husband placed one of these rings on her finger. The ancients thought that love traveled to the heart in the vein of the third finger of the left hand. To this day, that is still the finger that the wedding ring is worn on. To them, the circle indicated eternity and the iron symbolized lastingness. In any case, the bride received just one ring—upon her engagement. Then, in 1215 the Pope declared a longer waiting period between betrothal and the marriage. So, a second ring, the wedding ring, was placed on the bride's finger during the ceremony when she finally wed.

Another interesting legend is the ring ceremony. During the ceremony the ring was placed on the open Bible. The clergyman then sprinkled it with holy water and blessed it. Then the groom picked it up with his right hand and placed it on the bride's thumb, saying, "In the name of the Father." He then transferred it to the first finger, saying, "And of the Son." Next he changed it to the second finger as he said, "And of the Holy Ghost." Finally he placed it on her finger with "Amen." It did not seem to matter whether the ring was placed on the bride's right or left hand. Sometimes it was placed on the right hand at the espousal and on the left at the wedding ceremony.

Origin of the White Bridal Gown

In early Saxon days and through the 18th century, it was the poorer bride who came to her wedding dressed in a plain white robe. This was in the nature of a public statement that she brought nothing with her to her marriage and that therefore her husband was not responsible for her debts. Other brides simply wore their Sunday best. Red was a favorite during the Middle Ages in Europe. Icelandic brides chose black velvet. Colors were chosen for their symbolism as well as for preference. Blue meant constancy; green meant youth. Yellow signified jealousy and therefore was never worn. The brides of ancient Israel wore a blue ribbon on the shoulders of their robes to symbolize purity, fidelity and love. Over the years, the meaning of a white dress symbolized purity. Today, white merely symbolizes the wedding itself–and can be worn by anyone, including the second time and reaffirming bride.

Origin of the Bridal Veil

In Far Eastern countries, people believed that wicked spirits were especially attracted to women. So, as protection from the Evil Eye, women always wore veils. The custom continued although the feeling behind it changed with time into a role of modesty and obedience. From this the veil developed into a symbol of chastity. Then it became the sign of submission of women.

The introduction of the veil into Europe came through returning Crusaders. In early wedding traditions in Europe, the bride was bargained for through her father, was swathed in a bridal veil, and revealed to her mate after the ceremony!

In early centuries, Hebrew, Greek and Roman brides wore veils of many colors, and veils threaded with gold and on silver. In Southern Europe, early Christians placed a large cloth both the bride and groom. In Anglo–Saxon times, the bride wore her hair hanging loose as part of the wedding ritual. The Chinese held a sacred umbrella over the bride's head. Around 1500 in Europe, there was a fashionable conical headdress topped with a veil that hung to the toes. Each era has revealed a different style for the bridal veil.

Nellie Custis was the first American woman to wear a long, white veil of lace when she married Lawrence Lewis, an aide to President Washington. Nellie chose lace because the major had once glimpsed her face through the lace curtains of an open window–and then afterwards he couldn't stop telling her how beautiful she had looked!

The veil has traditionally stood for youth and virginity.

Origin of Throwing Rice, Old Shoes, etc.

In the days when people lived off the land, their existence depended upon having a good harvest and enough children to help with all the work. Primitive people believed the bride and groom spread gook luck on their wedding day. Anyone or anything that touched them would also be lucky. So they showered the couple with ripe grain or nuts, wishing a large harvest for themselves and a large family for the newly-weds. The throwing of grain seemed to symbolize good luck, fertility or abundance. To this day, wedding guests throw rice, grain, confetti, bird-seed, etc.

Among the ancient Assyrians and Jews, when a bargain was made, a man gave his sandal as an indication of good faith. A shoe was the symbol of authority. When the Anglo–Saxons hurled a shoe, it indicated that authority had been transferred. Some authorities believe that the throwing of a shoe can be traced back to the missiles that the bride's father hurled at the robber caveman.

Origin of Flowers for the Wedding Party

Throughout history, most celebrations of weddings used flowers in some way. Almost every country has its own traditions and symbolism concerning flowers.

Customs associate the orange blossom most closely with the wedding ceremony. The wearing of a wreath of orange blossoms as a crown over the bridal veil was a Saracen custom introduced by returning Crusaders. Orange blossoms were so expensive that only the wealthy could afford them and poorer brides resorted to artificial ones. A "kissing knot" of croton leaves and rosemary was hung over the bridal couple in Elizabethan

England. In Sweden it was believed necessary to put chives, garlic or rosemary in the bride's bouquet to deep the dwarfs from bothering her on her wedding day. In Poland it was believed that to sprinkle the bride's bouquet with sugar would keep her temper sweet. In Rome, roses and marigolds were used to decorate the bride's home. Below are some "meanings" associated with certain flowers:

Apple blossoms or quince blossoms–better things to come
Clematis–love vine
Ivy–good luck
Rosebud–a promise
Myrtle–lover's flower
Laurel–peace
Tulips–infidelity
Yellow flowers of any kind–jealousy
Orange blossoms–fertility
Heather and sweet basil–fortune
Baby's breath–fertility
Cabbage roses–richness of spirit
Anemones–hope
Lily of the Valley–happiness
Red and white roses–unity in love
Lilacs–youthful love
Pansies, forget–me–nots
White clover–special friendship

Origin of the Wedding Cake

The wedding cake has always been an important part of any wedding feast. Where or when it first originated cannot really be told since it is such an ancient custom. Among certain American Indian tribes, and among the Fiji Islanders, a bride offered her husband a cake of meal. The Romans broke a cake made of salted meal over the bride's head as a symbol of abundance, or fertility. Many people of various nations customarily dropped wheat, flour or cake upon the bride's head, then ate these offerings for good luck. The early Britons baked large baskets of small dry crackers for weddings, and every guest took one home–thus, the tradition of taking wedding cake home to "dream on." During the Middle Ages, it was traditional for the bride and groom to kiss over a pile of small cakes. The small cakes gradually increased in size and richness. Then an enterprising young baker decided to mass all these cakes together and cover them with frosting, thus the modern tiered wedding cake was born.

Cultural Customs

Every culture has its own charming wedding customs. Use your imagination and adapt one from the land of your ancestors. We've researched a few and a librarian will help you probe further.

Africa
"Mayst thou bear 12 children with him" is still the common salutation to brides in remote areas. Many tribes marry the couple by binding their wrists with plaited grass.

Afro–American
> On antebellum plantations, brides believed Tuesday and Wednesday weddings guaranteed them a good husband, long lives and happy days.

American Indian
> The groom wraps a woolen blanket around the bride to symbolize love and protection.

Bermuda
> Newlyweds plant a small tree in their garden. As it grows and strengthens, it symbolizes their love.

Belgium
> Brides carry a handkerchief embroidered with their name. After the ceremony, it's framed and displayed until the next family bride adds her name.

China
> Two goblets of honey and wine are joined with a red ribbon–the centuries–old color of love and joy–and the couple exchange a drink of unity.

Czechoslovakia
> Brides wear wreaths of rosemary for wisdom, love and loyalty.

England
> A country bride and her wedding party walk to church on a carpet of blossoms to assure a happy path through life.

Finland
> A bride once wore a golden crown during the ceremony. Later she was blindfolded while unmarried women danced around her. Whomever she crowned was predicted to be the next bride.

France
> The bride and groom drink a reception toast from an engraved silver two–handled cup, called a "coupe de marriage," and pass it on to future generations.

Germany
> On the eve of the wedding, friends of the bride smash pottery at her door. The loud noise is said to avert bad luck. To be sure of future bliss, the bride must sweep it up by herself.

Greece
> Couples hold candles decorated with ribbons and flowers.

Holland
> A bride and groom sit on thrones under an evergreen canopy – for everlasting love – during a pre–wedding party given by the family. One by one guests approach and offer good wishes.

India
> The groom's brother sprinkles flower petals on the couple at conclusion of the ceremony. Each family has prepared puffed rice which is mixed during the ceremony for prosperity and fertility.

Iran
> In Persian times, the groom bought ten yards of white sheeting to wrap around the bride as a wedding dress.

Ireland
> December 31 is considered the luckiest day for weddings in the Ould Sod.

Italy
> Since Roman times, couples have walked through the village passing out cakes and sweets.

Japan
> The bride and groom take nine sips of sake, becoming husband and wife after the first sip.

Israel
> For centuries, couples have had a marriage contract in the form of written vows, called a ketubbah, which is embellished by an artisan with bible verses and decorative borders symbolizing the home.

Lithuania
> Parents of the couple serve them symbols of married life: wine for joy, salt for tears, and bread for work.

Mexico
> A white silk cord is draped around the couple's shoulders to indicate their union. Later, guests hold hands in a heart–shaped circle while the newlyweds dance in the center.

Philippines
> The white silk cord custom is practiced here as well as in Mexico. All wedding expenses are met by the groom's family, who give the bride old coins symbolizing prosperity. The bride's family presents the newlyweds with a cash dowry.

Poland
> Brides wear embroidered white aprons over their gowns. Guests discreetly tuck money into the pockets of the aprons.

Rumania
> Wedding guests toss sweets and nuts at the couple to wish them prosperity.

Russia
> Wedding guests, other than family, receive gifts rather than give them.

Spain
> Brides wear mantillas and orange blossoms in their hair. Grooms wear a tucked shirt hand–embroidered by the bride.

Sweden
> Brides carry fragrant herb bouquets to frighten away trolls and grooms have thyme sewn into their wedding suits.

Switzerland
> Junior bridesmaids lead the procession tossing colored handkerchiefs to the guests. Whoever catches one contributes money for the couple's nest egg.

U.S.A.
> Early Americans gave the honeymooners posset, a hot drink of sweetened and spiced milk curdled with ale or wine, to keep up their energy.

Wales
> Brides give attendants cuttings of aromatic myrtle. When one blooms, it foretells another wedding.

Traditions

Trinkets of gold and silver (sometimes quite valuable) are wrapped in waxed paper or foil and often baked in one tier of the bride's cake, or inserted from the bottom after baking. These are intended only for the bridal party – the bridesmaid's gifts are on the left and groomsmen's are on the right.

Usually the bottom tier of the cake is used, and when the trinkets are placed inside, a marking such as an extra blossom bud, or a piece of white satin ribbon is used to indicate where the surprises are. Traditionally, the following "fortunes" are signified by each trinket:

For the bridesmaids:
Wishbone – luck
Heart – romance
Cat – old maid
Ring – next to marry
Dime – fortune
Thimble or miniature scissors – industrious

For the groomsmen:
A button or dog – bachelor
A man's wedding ring – next to marry
Gold coin – money
Dice – luck

Origin of Tossing the Bouquet or Garter

Originally, it was not a bouquet, but a garter that was tossed. This custom of tossing the garter originated in 14th Century France. For a time a stocking was tossed, but its removal was not easy or graceful. Finally some bride thought of tossing her bouquet and this custom has been followed ever since. Of course, to this day, the gal that catches the bouquet is predicted to be the next to marry, and the guy that catches the garter will be the next guy to get married!

Origin of the Honeymoon

The first marriages were by capture, not choice. When early man felt it was time to take a bride, he carried off an unwilling woman to a secret place where her parents or relatives wouldn't find them. While the moon went through all its phases – about 30 days – they hid from the searchers and drank a brew made from mead and honey. Therefore, we get the word honeymoon. Today, this has come to be a time for the couple to get away to relax and enjoy each other after the hectic schedule of preparing for the wedding.

Chapter 2

PLANNING THE SHOWER

As it should be with any kind of party, a bridal shower especially needs to be planned well in advance. It needs a great deal of thought and planning with special attention given to the bride and groom. The sky can be the limit, but I will say that successful bridal showers depend less upon the money spent than upon the creativity and ingenuity with which the party is planned. Look at it this way. If the host is having a good time planning and preparing the party, the shower guests, as well as the bride and groom will be having a good time too!

As I mentioned earlier, many things have changed over the years, but you must still be aware of the type of wedding, local customs, and the tastes and needs of the bride and groom. The number of showers given should be limited though. You want to avoid spending too much of the guest's money. You also should limit the guests to close friends, family, and wedding attendants. Never invite someone who is not invited to the wedding. Don't think that you are going to invite everyone on the wedding guest list, which often includes many acquaintances. This would be in very poor taste and is contradictory to the spirit of the traditional bridal showers. Those kind of situations make the bride and groom seem greedy for gifts and really ignore the closeness of the friendships for which a shower really is intended. The rule of thumb is one or two showers, but that can depend upon the types of showers and guests you are going to invite. Do not have showers too close to the wedding day because there are too many things for the bride and groom to take care of as their big day gets closer. One month or more before the wedding is soon enough. Considering that most weddings are planned at least 12 to 18 months prior, there is plenty of time to get going on planning a bridal shower, especially if seasons or climate are going to have an influence on your plans. The important point is that you set the date and put your creative thinking cap on.

Guests: Who Should Attend?

First of all, determine the size of your guest list by such considerations as space, the kind of service/menu you are planning, and whether this will be a large, informal party or an intimate gathering. The rule of thumb is roughly 15 people or so. As you read through the various themes in this book and choose the direction of the shower, you will have a good idea as to who and how many will be attending. The obvious point to remember here is that the guest list is only limited by remembering the shower is for the bride, groom, or couple. The host does not invite any personal friends unless they are friends and family of guests of honor or attendants in the wedding.

Invitations

The invitations should usually be sent about two weeks before the date of the event, but this is not a hard and fast rule. This depends upon the time of year and the type of shower you are giving. For certain themes, a simple telephone call will do. If it is a very formal affair that requires engraved invitations, you will need to allow more time for that. Likewise, some of the various themes have their own suggestions for invitations that include making your own.

Be sure to note <u>who</u> is hosting the shower and <u>where</u> the couple has registered for gifts on the invitation.

Menu

The menu will depend upon the theme of your shower. The ideas I have included in this book are mostly the very simple and easy to prepare foods. If you are having a formal shower, I recommend a more comprehensive cookbook that you can refer to. I just happen to be the type of person that enjoys fun dishes that are not time consuming thus creating a lot less stress.

Decorations

Practically anything goes whether simple or elaborate, depending upon the taste of the host or the theme of the shower. With party stores today, there is an unlimited amount of things that can be purchased above and beyond balloons, crepe paper, ribbons, and flowers. Many of the themes in this book offer suggestions for decorations that can be common household items. You'll find it amazing the props you have available right in your own backyard.

Entertainment

Although each of the various themes offer suggestions for some games and activities, you simply may not need them. It is always good to have some sort of an icebreaker prepared to get things going, but generally the theme itself or the guests themselves are sufficient. Some parties are dominated by conversation that games could actually spoil the fun. If you choose to have some games, prizes are optional. They should not be expensive, but should be neatly wrapped.

Host and Hostess Duties

Before we get into the purpose of this book, which is theme showers that are fun for the bride and groom, here is a quick summary of the DO'S and DON'TS of planning a wedding shower.

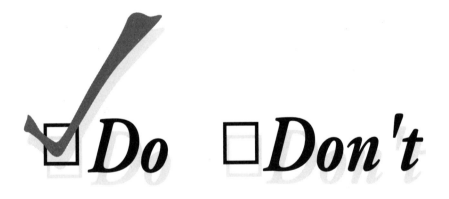

Wedding Shower DO'S and DON'TS

DO include the bride and groom whenever possible. WHY? because it's more fun, among many other reasons.

DO ask the bride and/or groom what type of shower they prefer. UNLESS, of course, it is a surprise.

DO note who is hosting the shower and where the couple is registered on the shower invitation, but NEVER on a wedding invitation.

DO determine the guest list with the bride or bride and groom.

DON'T charge the guests to attend.

DON'T invite guests to more than one shower.

DO invite immediate family and bridal attendants to all.

DON'T expect those who attend multiple showers to bring a gift to each shower. Unless, of course, it is a **no gift** shower

DON'T allow immediate family to host the shower.

DO consider group gifts for more expensive items.

DO assign someone to take photographs or video of the festivities to present to the bride and groom.

Bride, Groom: Guests of Honor

The guest(s) of honor should be attentive and considerate to not only the guests, but to the host as well. Guests of honor should arrive at least a half hour before the shower begins in order to assist the host and greet the guests as they arrive.

And no matter how busy they are in numerous other preparations, they should never forget to write thank–you notes for the gifts. Writing a special thank–you for the showers' host(s).

Guests' Duties

Just as the host, hostess, and bride have certain duties, the guests also are expected to fulfill certain obligations. Respond as quickly as possible upon receiving the invitation. If you decline, you should explain why. If you accept, only an emergency should prevent you from attending the shower. Upon accepting, you automatically agree to bring a gift. It does not need to be expensive, for it is the thought that really matters most. This does not excuse you from giving a wedding present assuming you have received an invitation to the wedding.

Try to be very close to ON TIME. It is not a good idea to arrive early as to interfere with the host or hostess. Park where you are not blocking a driveway or street so that other guests will have room to park. It is not proper to assist the host unless you are specifically asked to do so. Unwanted help can be very frustrating or even offensive.

Try very hard to participate in conversation and activities. It helps everyone to be more at ease. Do not overstay your welcome. Be sure to call the hostess a day or two later to express your appreciation.

Chapter 3

THEMES, GIFTS, AND ENTERTAINMENT THAT MAKE THE PARTY

A specific theme simplifies planning, providing a focal point for all the party elements. Special days/holidays (Christmas, Valentine's Day, Easter. Fourth of July, etc.) have simple, colorful built–in themes. Endless opportunities exist for festive affairs. Themes for these varied occasions may be keyed to the seasons or to the purpose of the gathering, or even to a favorite hobby or avocations of the person for whom the celebration is being given. The hostess and the bride and/or groom select a mutually convenient date, and then decide what kind of shower is most appropriate. See chapter 7 for a guide and check-list for planning your shower.

Antique & Heirloom Shower

This shower is unique because none of the gifts are new. The antiques or heirloom shower is an opportunity for the family members to get together for the purpose of presenting collectibles to the bride and groom. It is also a special time for the family to share memories. The families gather together in a celebration to exchange memories, momentous, and family treasures for future safekeeping.

One very important point that must be addressed in a shower such as this, is to consider whether or not the couple has a pre-nuptial agreement.

It is an issue that should be discussed in order to protect these kinds of gifts. You obviously want these special kinds of gifts to remain with the proper side of the "family". A pre-nuptial agreement can spell out that these gifts are to stay with the family from which they were given. A family attorney should be advised on this and other ways to protect family heirlooms. See page 68, Protecting your wedding gifts and other valuables.

The activity for this shower is focused on the gifts. As each family member presents their gift, they should give a brief history or story relating to the gift and it's origin. It would also be nice to have a family photo album and/ or home movies for everyone to look at and remember.

You may want to have a simple sit-down family dinner or just beverages and snacks. Whichever one you think will provide the most relaxed way for everyone to share the memories and conversation.

Around the World Shower or Heritage Shower

This is the shower that is really based upon what type of food you want to serve and then to coordinate the decorations, music, and activities that go along with that. Following are some examples to give you some basic ideas.

German

The name for this shower should really be Octoberfest - just as you imagine it would be in Germany. The bride would be the *fräulein* and the groom the *herr*. You could even suggest that your guests come dressed in traditional dresses with aprons for the gals and lederhosen or shorts with suspenders for the guys. The decorations would include any autumn leaves and other flowers filled with fall colors. Perhaps you could include some beer steins or other items of German tradition. Play some polka and accordion waltz music to put everyone in the festive German spirit. Serve bratwurst, sauerkraut, and German potato salad with, or course, plenty of beer.

Offer a toast *"Hein Prosit"* (To your health) or *"Ofen warm, Bier Kalt, Weib Jung, Wein alt"* (Oven warm, beer cold, wife young, wine old).

Hawaiian/ Jamaican/ Dominican

Individually or collectively, these Carribean themes portray a beach setting and luau type of music with dancing. Your neighborhood library is sure to have some music you can rent to provide the perfect mood. Perhaps even some Don Ho. The food is simple. Definitely lots of fresh fruit and as much variety as you can think of. You may also want to serve smoked salmon or a roasted pig. Ask your guests to wear flowered shirts, skirts, and straw hats.

Offer a toast *"Hauoli maoli oe"* (To your happiness).

Irish

With an Irish theme, be sure that your guests come with a few prepared toasts and even some Irish drinking songs. Here again, your local library can be a valuable source for ideas and music. Ask your guest to wear lots

of green and, hopefully, no one will show up wearing the dreaded orange. The food can be as simple as corned beef and cabbage. Serve lots of beer with some after dinner drinks like Irish creme...
"Erin Go Bragh". (God go with you).

Italian

This is the shower that would my favorite because I love pasta and I love to eat. You could serve a salad, spaghetti or lasagna, and spumoni ice cream or Italian pastries for desert. Be sure to have plenty of wine on hand and a variety of fresh breads. Some music suggestions might be Frank Sinatra and the decorations might include pictures of the "rat pack". You might ask your guests to dress in gangster and mob attire.
"Viva l'amor!" (Long live love).

Mardi Gras

As you can imagine, this is the shower New Orleans style. A local travel agent can supply you with some posters for the backdrop, then just add lots and lots of color. Have your guests dress in flashy, gaudy attire accented with the traditional bead necklaces. Don't forget to have them don a Mardi Gras masquerade mask. You might even be fortunate to have a costume rental shop in your area. Play a variety of jazz music from blues to some contemporary Al Jureau.

The food for this is anything Cajun style. Some ideas are boiled shrimp, fish, crawfish or fresh oysters in the shell. You can also make a variety of dishes that simply need some hot, Cajun seasoning added to them. Beverages can range from ice tea to margaritas in a blender or beer.

Mexican

If you're a lover of all kinds of Mexican food, the hotter the better -
then this is the shower for you. You can make this one a very simple
preparation by providing a make-your-own taco, burrito, or salad by setting up a buffet style food table. Offer a variety of shells, then put out
bowls filled with meat, lettuce, cheese, olives, jalapeño peppers, vegetables, sour cream, salsa hot sauce, and whatever else you can imagine. Add
some tortilla chips with dips. You will definitely want to offer some
sparkling water, beer, and a variety of margaritas blended with real fruit.
All of which can be made non-alcoholic if desired. Ice cream makes for an
ideal desert.

An activity for this shower could include a piñata, which can really be a
lot of fun. You could also ask your guests to dress casual, but be sure to
include a big sombrero-hat. "*Salud!*" (To your health).

Norwegian

Although you can live anywhere to put on this kind of shower, it seems
to be much more popular in the Midwest. The Scandinavian menu here
is much more defined. Lutefisk, a specially prepared fish, is unique in fla-
vor and not advised if your guests have never eaten it before. Swedish
meatballs, gravy, and mashed potatoes are always good. You must have
lefse complimented with butter and/or sugar. (See recipe section for lefse
roll-ups) The Norwegians are also noted for numerous specialty deserts
such as rosettes, sandbakkelse, krumkake, and homemade pies. Fresh
baked bread will top it all off. The recommended beverage for this menu
is lots of really good coffee and condiments.

Generally the favorite activity is relaxing conversation. Perhaps if you have a good-natured group of guest you can tell Ole and Lena and Sven jokes or stories. This is also a shower where you need not be afraid to ask your guests to bring a favorite traditional dish to pass. They love to cook.

Oriental

This shower's activity could be including your guests in all of the cooking. Have several of your guests bring a wok. Arrange a large cooking area. Provide all of the fixings, let your guests help cut them up, and the rest is a simple stir-fry plus prepared rice. Be sure to supply plenty of fortune cookies or perhaps you could make your own with humorous fortunes inside. You might also want to invent a chopsticks eating contest. It would be great if you could arrange an area where the guests could sit on pillows to eat around a lowered table that easily is invented. The attire for this shower can be made fun as well. Just round up several bathrobes with homemade colorful, satin-type belts. Hand your guests their ready-made Kimono, add Chinese flute music and you're off to a good start. Decorate with a variety of fresh flowers and bird ornaments.

The beverage for stir-fry can be saki or any kind of wines. Definitely include sparkling water with cold and hot tea.

"*Konotabi wa omedeto gozaimasu*" (Congratulations to the bride and groom).

Roman Toga

When in Rome, do as the Romans do. Inform your guests that they will have to make their own toga to wear made simply out of old, white bed sheets. Tie with a belt and load up with lots of old, gaudy jewelry. Do an invitation that is clearly Caesar and Cleopatra.

The menu is any kind of food, just as much variety as possible. Don't forget the grapes and other fresh fruit. Keep the wine flowing.

Backyard, Patio, Pool, or Hot Tub Shower

For friends of the couple
a day in the sun.
We'll meet at the pool (or backyard or hot tub, etc.)
for lots of fun.
Bring your suit and hat
as we splash and swim,
This party will last
until the daylight dims.

Although this shower clearly suggests an outdoor event, you can also rent some rooms at a local hotel that provides a pool, hot tub, sauna, and the like. These facilities may let you bring your own food in or they may prefer to provide it for you. You could also order a specialty food, like pizza, to be delivered to you. Just be sure to inquire about the reservation dates well in advance.

If you're going to go the backyard route, pray for good weather or have an option available such as an indoor patio, garage or tent. Set up the barbecue grill and you are basically ready to go. When you are hosting a party such as this it is best to keep the menu simple. I suggest you stick to hamburgers, hot-dogs, bratwurst, chicken, or shish kabobs that can be ready to cook when the grill and guests are ready to eat. It is best to cook something that is quick to make or can cook slowly with very little attention. Throw out a variety of snacks, veggies with dips, salads, and fruit. Desert could even be fruit, such as slices of watermelon or perhaps a watermelon boat filled a mixture of fruits.

Next, ask your guests to help by providing some large coolers. You fill them up with a variety of beverages. Add the ice and your guests can serve themselves. You may want to ask your guests to bring additional lawn chairs if you don't have enough. Be sure when you set up the area for the party that you also provide enough shade or umbrellas.

Bring out the boom box, play some music, blow up some inflatable pool toys or rafts, and let the party begin. Some activities might be volleyball, croquette, a friendly poker game, horseshoes, lawn darts, or a host of others.

Bar Shower

This is the shower for couples who have a traditional or favorite pub/saloon that they frequently meet at. And, naturally, you hold the shower at this social establishment. Most of the informal taverns will allow you to bring in some food or pay the owner to set something up for you or simply have it catered in. Keep the menu light by offering snacks, dips, sandwiches with cold cuts or hot beef or sloppy joes, and a few simple hors d' oeuvres. The entertainment is already there with music, pool tables, darts, card playing, and video games. This one also comes complete with a bartender/waitress to serve everyone's favorite beverages. You may even want to offer some limited beverages at the host's expense.

Of course the perfect gifts for a bar shower are recreation room/bar room accessories. Decanters, ice buckets, wine glasses, tumblers, shot glasses, specialty gifts to hang on the walls, conversation pieces, bar stools, hanging lights, CD player, television, a VCR, various tapes, bottles of wine, a favorite liqueur, blender, and a how-to-book for mixing up a variety of cocktails.

You will want to host this party at a time of the day when the bar is not busy though so that you have the entire place mostly to yourself. Play some background music, have a gift opening, share some laughs and conversation, and have fun. The invitations could be as fun as writing the information on the inside of a matchbook that advertises the particular bar and mailing or handing them out.

Barn Party Shower

This shower is tailored around the old-fashioned barn party of years ago. Today, many couples are actually forming their own co-op to help each other year-round. It is as simple as each member offering a specific talent for repairs and improvements. This can actually be ideal for a couple that has just purchased a home or other living quarters. A home needing some TLC. The guests' gift is to provide some sort of services that the couple needs done or you may just plan a day or weekend that the guests will show up with their sleeves rolled and ready to work. The host should be sure to help the couple provide a list of things to do and match talents as best as possible.

If you really think about it, you will find that in today's world everyone has some kind of talent to offer. Even if the guest is not very handy or mechanically inclined, they can assist in preparing a meal, taxes, cleaning or planting flowers. Perhaps the others can decorate, do yard work, refinish furniture, wallpaper, paint, assist in moving, or even a major project like building a deck or garage.

You will want to serve a very light lunch, however you will definitely want a nice, hearty meal at the end of tiring work day with as much celebration as their sore backs can handle.

Basket Shower

A tisket a tasket
a big and fancy basket...

The invitations for this shower must spell out that each guest is to bring a gift in a basket or a gift that is a basket. Baskets have always been a favorite decorating idea to hang or put things in. The ideas are endless - bread basket, waste basket, wicker paper plate holders, wicker trays, a laundry basket, hamper, a basket filled with decorator soaps or guest towels for the bathroom, silk flower arrangements, or just a unique basket. How about a picnic basket filled with accessories, a gardening basket filled with a couple of tools, a wine and cheese basket, or a music basket filled with tapes, CDs, or videos. I'm sure you get the hang of it...no pun intended.

Bridal Shower

History tells us that the purpose of the shower has always been to shower the bride with gifts. This book, however primarily directs the gifts to couples. What I refer to here as a bridal shower focuses on gifts the bride, groom, or bride and groom have registered for. In the case with all showers, but NOT wedding invitations, you may be specific in the invitation as to where the guests of honor have registered. This shower is not only very practical in order to avoid duplicating gifts, but is generally a more formal, yet a very traditional shower. It's great for the guests that may not know each other, it is helpful for couples that might be difficult to buy for, and there is generally a formality to it that allows for the most inexperienced host to feel comfortable.

The format is to greet the guests, serve a beverage, perhaps play some old fashion party games, eat a meal together, provide a gift opening time, some more friendly conversation, and then ending the party at a pre-scheduled time.

You may still choose a theme for this, but be specific on the invitation about the theme including the gift.

Broads, Brutes, & Mutts Shower

I like the name of this shower as it is really intended for an older bride and groom-to-be or an older couple that has married before. It is intended to mean that the couple may bring their children...and/or a pet. For couples that have been friends for many years and enjoy getting everyone together, this is just a simple shower. Perhaps no theme is needed, or each guest brings a dish to pass and some beverages. Put your thinking cap on and be creative....motorcycle groups, camping groups, etc.

Camper's Delight Shower

I love to go camping and so do lots of our friends. It just makes sense to throw a shower at a group campsite. Even with some friends that aren't really campers, you can usually convince them to go along for a night or a weekend. It is not difficult to round up a few extra tents or bunk together in a camping trailer. You may even want to make a small road trip out of this and find a resort where you can rent cabins.

The activities here are obvious by taking advantage of nature itself. Fishing, swimming, cookouts, campfires with sing-a-longs and stories, and lots of relaxation. You want to make sure that you set aside a special time specifically for the shower and gift opening. If your couple happens to be campers, the gifts will be any camping accessory you can think of. If they aren't really campers, pick gifts that are somehow related to the outdoors. Look at the ideas under the Backyard Shower. You could also do a "Christmas in July" party (see holiday showers and picnic shower). The menu is going to be anything you can make on a barbecue grill or outdoor fire. I suggest that each couple be assigned a meal to prepare for the day or weekend. One couple can do breakfast, one lunch, another dinner, and so on.

If the couple happens to be older or even a second marriage with children, you may want to consider this a family event. Of course, if you include children, make sure there are plenty of activities for kids at your particular camp.

Casino Party Shower

Even if your guests have never been to Las Vegas or Atlantic City, they are sure to have fun at this shower – especially if the guests of honor and friends like to gamble.

It is very easy to rent the equipment and all of the necessary playing materials. Then gather some volunteers that are willing to play casino. If you need to, you can borrow card tables and chairs. Get out the play money and we're off.

The backdrop for this theme speaks for itself. The menu should be very limited. Just serve some snacks and beverages. Provide a couple of servers to wait on your guests. They will all feel like they in a real casino, especially if the piles of play money start stacking up.

The gifts to the bride and groom-to-be can be almost anything here. One great idea is to send the couple on a vacation to Las Vegas or any other gambling resort. There are many exciting packages now available through travel agencies. If the couple is planning to get married in Las Vegas (75,000 each year) this is still a nice send off.

It would also be fun to have the guests dress in glitzy attire with lots of flash or maybe a Bugsy Seagal, mobster appeal.

Craft Shower

Some brides-to-be and their friends might be very craft orientated. This makes for generally fun, hands-on activity. Ask each guest to bring a craft or hobby they are working on. Share ideas and examples with each other. The gift to the couple is something that is handmade.

Perhaps also, there is a new craft that your guests would like to learn. You, as the host, may be able to teach them or consider bringing in an instructor from a hobby or craft shop that would be delighted to share their talent. One example was a couple that loved ceramic ornaments. The guests all enrolled in a ceramic class together. They picked out a variety of indoor and outdoor projects to do. By the end of the class, they had a finished ornament to give to the couple as their gift. It was really a fun gathering as well. For a girls only shower, how about an old fashioned quilting bee?

Cupid's Shower

Roses are red
violets are blue,
She said, He said
"I Love You Too!"
Come share in a valentine
shower for two.
Just weeks before
they'll be saying "I DO!"

This is obviously a romantic shower. If you can't remember what that means, watch the video movie of Romeo & Juliet again. My memories are of the old fashioned parties we had at school when we were kids. The invitations could be simple, inexpensive children's valentines or handmade with crayons and this little verse above. Maybe a heart with an arrow through it with John loves Mary or the couple's initials carved inside a heart.

The decorations are cupids, hearts, paper wedding bells, balloons, and streamers in red and white or pink. Think love foods for your menu. Heart shaped pizza, cookies, and cakes. Finger sandwiches with a variety of toppings and cut-out like hearts with a cookie cutter. Don't forget the valentine party favors filled with those candy hearts that have romantic little messages on them. Add delicious red punch.

If you are inviting couples, how about playing the Newlywed game? You can purchase it at a local toy store. If its girls only, romantic tales about their mates. Just like the traditional slumber party. Include some romantic music or maybe a piano player. The gifts could be anything romantic.

Dress to the Nines Shower

As the theme suggests, this shower is formal wear material. That is suit and tie, and dressy gowns. The invitations should be engraved or at least look engraved. They should include R.S.V.P.'s and mailed or hand-delivered. Leave no stone unturned, this is first class all the way. To many couples, this is an opportunity to get dressed up...like going to the prom. To other couples, it may be the only type of shower they will accept.

The setting for this shower will be a beautiful home, private club, or upscale restaurant. Perhaps even pick up the guests in a rented limousine. This can be a formal lunch or dinner, but the key is formal. This means the best dinnerware/china, linen napkins, crystal glassware, and elegant centerpieces or decorations. The menu should be at least three courses. Serve wine and/or champagne. Soft background music is most appropriate. The activity is conversation. You may even want to include a cocktail hour before the meal.

Engagement Shower/Party

This shower is specifically held to formally announce the engagement of a couple. The invitations should clearly state that. The invitations should also tell the guests whether or not a gift is appropriate. I think the best way to do that is to word it as such - In lieu of a gift, please prepare a toast to offer Mary and John (the bride and groom-to-be). The gifts should be fairly general, such as picture frames, music box, table top books, figurines, flower vase, etc.

In situations where the family and friends of the guests of honor have not met before or in a case where the bride-to-be and the groom-to-be do not live in the same city or state, it is a great opportunity to bring everyone together for the first time. This shower should be discussed with the guests of honor beforehand. They should be very involved in where the shower will be held, the type of shower it will be, and especially in coordinating the invitation list with addresses. A video of this is especially nice because of the variety of special toasts by family and friends.

Family Reunion Shower

This shower is for relatives
Come one - come all!
As the families unite
and answer this call.
Let's welcome this couple
into our fold.
Sharing the love for
our families to hold.

In some respects, this is like an engagement shower. The exception is that this shower is tailored around a family reunion. It actually may mean having two showers – one with Mary's side of the family and one with John's side of the family. It is a unique opportunity for everyone to meet one another. The best part of this shower is that most of the planning is done and the reunion committee has already made most of the preparations. The menu is traditionally a dish to pass. You must let the guests know, however that there is to be a gift involved. Perhaps they simply go in together on one special gift. I recommend that a formal announcement be made by the bride and/or groom-to be and allow everyone to offer a casual toast. Be sure to have someone taking pictures. What a terrific way to start off a scrapbook. Better yet, take a video.

As this poem suggests, you could even try to get both sides of the families together for a reunion. Even if it is only the most immediate of family. If you should decide to go that route, be sure to have nametags for everyone and a guest book. This is something that each family will remember for years to come.

Gadget and Widget Shower

As time goes on, it seems that there are still new ideas everyday. Some are just a re-invention of the mousetrap and others are truly unique and useful. Some people love anything new and different. And we all know about those people who are difficult to buy for or those that just seem to already have everything. So, you guessed it. This is the shower where the guests bring any kind of a gift that is a gadget or widget. It is fun just to watch the bride and groom-to-be open their gifts. There should be a little story to go with each of these gadgets and widgets and, in some cases, at least an explanation of what they are or what they are used for. Some easy ideas are kitchen accessories. I recently purchased a modern potato peeler that makes peeling fun. There are also electronic peelers now. How about that tool that slices a radish so it looks like a rose? The info-commercials on television or web sites on computers are great resources for interesting ideas. Perhaps you could get your guests together ahead of time to share ideas and decide who will buy what. It seems hard to believe they could receive duplicates at this shower, but it is possible. Keep this shower casual with a simple menu. The activity is the gifts themselves.

Gardening Shower

This theme can be taken in a variety of ways. My friend Kay, has the most beautiful backyard garden and deck that is immersed in flowers, ornaments, birdhouses, butterfly houses, a gazebo, park bench, and... well you get the idea. The point here is that you might simply want to have a shower in the garden with the food and beverages served outdoors. Or you may have a couple that loves to garden or do landscape decorating. In this case the gifts are the focus of the theme. There are many gift ideas to choose from – such as those at my friend Kay's or pottery, gardening tools/accessories, lawn ornaments, water fountains, unique hanging baskets, how-to-books on the subject of gardening (and there are many) or a subscription to similar type of magazine.

You could even take the direction of giving live plants, flowers, shrubs, vines, and other items that you actually bring to plant for the couples part of their gift. Obviously the setting for this would at the guests of honor's home. Include wind chimes, sun catchers, birdhouses, landscape lights, decorator flags, and silk flower centerpieces for the patio table.

The dress should be casual, the menu simple, and held outdoors if possible- but not necessary. Use your imagination.

Holiday Showers

As these themes suggest, the calendar is your primary guide. Some are very traditional times of the year and some are just meant to be fun and more non-traditional. Following are few suggestions:

April Fools Shower

A fun, prank-filled, and full of surprises shower.

Christmas Shower

A perfect opportunity shower because family and friends are already available to get together. It is especially a nice time to meet up with old high school friends who may be in town for the holiday. The perfect gift here is to have each guest bring a special Christmas ornament for the couple to someday share on their first married Christmas and the long lasting memories in the years to come.

Easter Shower

Let's have an Easter Egg/ gift hunt for this one. Perhaps even a scavenger hunt. See the game section further on in this book.

Halloween Shower

How about a masquerade party or costume ball? Fill the activity sheet with an apple bobbing or pass an apple from guest to guest by their necks. Decorate haunted house style.

July 4th Shower

Fireworks and firecrackers. A cake with sparklers. A backyard barbecue or a camper's delight theme. Lots of red, white and blue.

Labor Day Shower

A picnic, a boat outing, a gathering on the beach somewhere.

May Day Shower

Think spring and lots of flowers.

Memorial Day Shower

Similar to Labor Day.

New Years Day/ Eve Shower

What a way to bring in the new year. Noise makers, hats, and Auld Lang Syne.

St. Patrick's Day Shower

Same as Irish Shower.

Thanksgiving Shower

Like the Christmas Shower, a great time to seize the opportunity for old friends and family to get together. Just don't forget to add the turkey with all of the trimmings.

Valentine's Day Shower

Same as a Cupid's Shower.

Home Improvement Party Shower

For the bride or groom
and couples too,
This shower's for hardware
whether old or new.
Bring a gadget or a tool
for their household repair,
So they won't borrow your tools
in their time of despair.

This is one of the most popular showers today. With bachelor and stag parties becoming different than they used to be, this is a perfect way to include both masculine and feminine ideas. I found that most of the major hardware chain stores offer a bride and groom registry. The gift ideas are endless and provide for totally practical, useful necessity items. They are generally things that most couples forget about as well. In fact, I know many women who were thrilled at receiving a basic tool set, step ladder, brooms, scissors, batteries, kerosene lamps, mops, picture hanging kits, rakes, shovels, and the like. I also know some couples who are really handy and were happy to receive a gift like portable, battery operated tools —caulking guns, skill saws, nailing guns, sanding tools, etc.

These gifts wouldn't even have to be wrapped. Present them to the couple as if you were watching the television show "Home Improvement" with a real tool time gal or guy. Perhaps you, as the host, might want to wear a pair of bib coveralls. Tell your guests to dress very casual. An ideal location for this shower would be a garage. Use some sawhorses with a board across them for your food table...get the idea?

"Home Party" Shower

The purpose of this shower is to watch someone present their products or to provide a demonstration for them. Generally, the gifts are then purchased from a catalog. Though this shower is hosted like any other shower, the representative for whose products they represent will share ideas and may offer any specials deals they have at that time. If they also offer special, free gifts to the host of the party, they should be given to the guest-of-honor. The guests often enjoy these parties because they can purchase items they want or need for themselves as well. It is also a simple and easy shower to put together.

Be sure to have a room that will be large enough for everyone to sit in while viewing the presentation and also an area to display the products being offered. Once everyone has placed their orders, provide food that will be easy to eat from their lap. You could also have this shower without the guest-of-honor.

There are several kinds of "home" showers being offered today. Some examples are Tupperware, Amway, Mary Kay, Avon, and many new mail order catalog types of companies. Consider a makeover for the guest of honor if you are offering cosmetic products. There are decorating companies that feature wall hanging products for every room in the house. Perhaps a simple personal shower for the bride-to-be. You can get ideas from your friends or check the yellow pages of your telephone directory.

Honeymoon Shower

Bon Voyage!

This shower promotes gifts the couple will need to take on their honeymoon – depending upon where they will be going. Or if the couple has registered with a travel agency that offers a registry and specializes in honeymoon packages, the gift may be the honeymoon itself. The guests go in together to purchase airfare, hotel, or the package. If that is the case, have the travel agent provide posters and pictures of the honeymoon destination and use them for your decorations.

The gifts might otherwise include luggage, camera, film, photo album, matching bathrobes, beach towels, or more specific items tailored to their destination. This type of shower has most recently become popular because of the burden of expense for many couples or simply because the couple may already have the many basic material gifts.

Honeymoon Is Over Shower

This can be a great surprise shower for the couple when they return from their honeymoon. It is especially appropriate for the couple who eloped or held their wedding at an out-of-town location. The couple will be pleasantly surprised by this terrific "Welcome Home" type of celebration. This shower should take place relatively soon after the wedding, but take into consideration that they may be tired from traveling and probably worn out on restaurant eating. A relaxed and home-style meal would be nice. The easiest way to pull this one off is to invite the couple over for dinner and encourage them to bring photos and souvenirs from their trip. The invitations could be any type of postcard that has some sort of romantic photo or simple arrange by telephone.

Decorate with a WELCOME HOME or JUST MARRIED sign. Get ready to shout a loud "SURPRISE!". The activity here is conversation and the highlights of their honeymoon.

Let's Go To the Oscars Party Shower

To set the stage for this one, just watch the Emmy, Golden Globe, or Oscars Awards on television. Pretend it is a Hollywood Premier. Make your guests-of-honor the stars of the movie titled "This Is Your Life". The story line of this script is about how they met and the romance that followed. You may even include a mock wedding as the ending of your movie. Ask each of the guests to dress as their favorite movie stars fitting them in the screen play with real parts to read or memorize. Have your guests-of-honor read the script you have prepared for them. Hire someone to film the movie on a video camera.

After the guests have watched their own premier movie, the host should hand out awards to all of the actors and actresses (guests). Make up some of your own awards. Find some old trophies and convert them into Oscars. Be sure to add this to your previous movie film at the end. Then have the videographer put his or her creativity to work with some music, sound effects, title, and credits onto the film.

While taking a break before the awards, provide hors d 'oeuvres and beverages. This makes it easier for the guests to eat and drink while mingling with each other. It also makes it more fun for the guest to play their Hollywood parts. The gifts could a variety of classic movies on video for the couple to snuggle up to.

Linen Shower

A linen shower features towels, washcloths, bath mats, shower curtains, bedspreads, sheets, pillow cases, comforters, blankets, napkins, table cloths, placemats, and anything else that is found in a linen closet. If the bride has registered for any of these kinds of gifts, it makes the buying much easier. Otherwise, it is a good idea to ask her what her favorite colors are or stick to neutral color themes. You should also find out bed sizes, pillow sizes, etc. It is the hosts' responsibility to know these things and to inform the guests.

As you may already know, linens have become quite costly these days. That is why these are gifts that are always appreciated, and often needed, by the bride and groom-to-be.

For your decorations, be sure to use your best linens wherever possible. Add some beautiful centerpieces, dinnerware, and fresh flowers or lighted scented candles.

Lingerie Shower

Lingerie showers typically have been for women only. If it is, you should only include the bride-to-be's closest friends and family because it is considered an intimate shower. The bride-to-be's sizes and color preferences should be included with the invitations. You may want to consider hosting a lingerie style show, as there are a variety of these companies available today with their own models. If you choose that option, feel free to invite couples and give all of you guests an opportunity to buy themselves a gift. These are fun, yet allow you to bring the shopping right to your home if you so desire.

Gowns, robes, slips, hosiery, lingerie cases, sachets, teddy bear sets, penoires, pajamas, and other personal items are some of the many gift ideas.

The decorations should present a soft atmosphere. Work with pastels such as pink, yellow, peach, pale blue, and white for colors. Another nice touch might be a gift of a small chest of drawers with ribbons on the handles. Place the gifts inside the half-open drawers and on top.

Love Bus, Love Train, Love Plane, or Love Boat Shower

This shower requires quite a bit of advance planning because you will need to charter one of these described modes of transportation. As I have been on a few Love Buses, I will use that as my example. A date is set and the bus with driver is chartered. The destination is an overnight trip and the destination is a mystery to all of the guests. Each of the guests pays for their portion of the trip, but it is free to the guests-of-honor. It is a couple's only trip.

Several little stops are made along the way ending at a nice hotel/resort with lots of built in activities -swimming, golf, restaurants, etc.

During the bus ride, each guest receives a half of a valentine. At one of the stops, the guests are asked to seek out the person who has the other half of the valentine. When you find that person, you then sit with them on the bus to the next stop. This encourages new conversation and laughter. Typically, there are also other couples on the bus that are considering marriage. Thus at the ultimate destination, some funny mock weddings are performed. It is filled with lots of fun...thank-you Sue and Jim Moore of La Crescent, MN.

As you can see, this idea can be extended to trains, planes, and boats.

Millennium 2000 Shower

This is the only open-ended shower of the book. The shower of the century has yet to be determined for the next generation is just arriving. I imagine it to be very futuristic. Please send me your ideas.

Forties Shower

Sinatra, Bing Crosby......ask your grandparents.

Fifties Shower

Sock hop, poodle skirts, the jitterbug, and Elvis.......ask your parents.

Sixties Shower

Flower power, political demonstrations, love and peace, the Beatles.....think back.

Seventies Shower

You are the baby boomers...so you ought to know.

Eighties Shower

Apple computers, science fiction, the emergence of speed and technology.

Nineties Shower

A reflection of the last 10 years......what was important to you?

Money Shower

The gifts for this shower are to be money, and may be coins or currency in various denominations. A money tree is fun and simple to make. Just find a nice tree branch and spray it silver, gold, white, leave it natural, or whatever. Anchor the branch to look like a tree in some sort of container with Styrofoam to hold it in place. Turn each guest's gift of money into an ornament by attaching ribbons and hanging them on the tree. You could also place the money inside of a colored envelope with the name of the giver and a brief message on the outside. Then attach it with a ribbon and tie on to the tree.

At this shower, however, the guests-of-honor do not open the gifts. They simply take the "money tree" home with them. The host then provides a group greeting card or guest book signed by each guest that is then presented to the bride and groom.

Mood Shower

Some people call this a candlelight shower. Well, candlelight plus romance equals mood. This can be an elegant evening, sit-down dinner with lots of candles lit or a casual, sit on pillows evening with a pizza. Just be sure to have as many candles as the room can handle and be careful to have them safely placed. Play some tasteful, quieter, romantic music in the background to set the mood. Offer wine and conversation.

The gifts for this couples' shower would be candles, candle holders, wine, floor pillows, wine glasses....anything that effects your mood.....romantic mood, that is!

On A Scale of One-To-Ten Shower

Happiness is being a dieter...and marrying one.
Marriage is like fitness...forever.
Live on Fitness and Love.
Two can live cheaper than one...especially dieting.

This idea comes from my friends at a fitness center that I belong to. It relates to anyone who is working at some sort of healthy exercise, diet, or fitness. In fact, your guests may well be a group of people that workout together. No matter what level anyone is at in their particular program, the bond is a common one where the need for encouragement is critical. You can even extend this theme to a golf group, softball team, aerobics class, weight watchers support group, and variety of other athletic groups.

You can host this shower wherever the group usually meets or a coffee shop that serves yogurt, mineral water, juices, fruits, and other low calorie items.

The gifts here may be encouragement in itself or a basket filled with tea, fruit, bath oils, poetry, and things that work to enhance the spirit. You may want to give a group gift that is a membership to a fitness center or health club. One of the best gifts a friend of mine once received was a book about the power of Zen. It literally changed her life.

Paper Shower

There are many useful items needed by a bride and groom that are made of paper. The gifts to bring to this shower would include: stationary, calendars, memo pads, playing cards, paper money (currency or check), desk blotters, monogrammed napkins or coasters, or towels, facial tissues with a decorator container, placemats, picnic accessories that include paper plates and holders, etc. Even newspaper and magazine subscriptions, or books are acceptable. There are so many new and contemporary gifts on the market that qualify such as a framed print, paper flowers, oriental fans, or paper maché conversation pieces just to name a few.

Personal Shower

The personal shower is similar to a lingerie shower except that the gift items are expanded to include jewelry, cosmetics, perfume, manicure accessories, gloves, hats, umbrellas, and anything else that is exclusively for the bride itself. I think a shower like this ought to be a good old fashioned slumber party with the girls?!

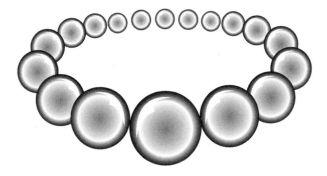

"Play It Again, Sam" or Second Time Around Shower

Though they did this once before
and it didn't work out,
It's the second time around
that will really count.
They found love at last
and a future abound,
To form a new kind of past
in their happiness found.

You guessed it. For couples in a second wedding. Anything goes here. Although it might be fun to give the couple used items that the guests no longer need, yet might make practical gifts for the couple. Perhaps have the guests go in together on something they would like to have. Generally gifts are not required here.

Some couples never had a big wedding the first time, so they like having a big wedding and showers the second time. Either way, the couples are usually older, therefore, making the decision of the type of shower you want to give relatively simple.

This is also a nice way to thank the many friends and family who were supportive in the past.

Pound Party Shower

This shower is weighed by the pound
with gifts the couple needs around.
-a pound of nails and hammer set
- a pound of nuts and nutcracker set
- a pound of coffee and a coffeemaker
- a pound of paper and a pen set
- a pound of flour and a breadmaker

That's the idea, you can take it from there. Just scope out the grocery store, hardware store, drug store, or stationary store. The list is longer than you think. Maybe you can think of some funny phrases to go with your gift that relates to love somehow.

Recipe Shower

Bring a recipe
and a favorite dish,
This is a shower
You won't want to miss.
This one's for those
who love to gourmet,
Let's eat and celebrate
their near wedding day.

This idea could also be used with the family reunion shower. I like it best to share a recipe or meal idea that can be made for two. This is also great for families of different ethnic backgrounds because it can offer an opportunity to learn and taste other cultural dishes.

A great gift idea here might also be a cookbook from each of the families with their own respectively favorite recipes.

Rock-Around-The-Clock Shower

This shower centers around giving gifts to the couple that are specifically used at different times of the day. In fact, the invitation should provide a basic list of ideas to bring across the theme. The following is very basic and meant to be general.

8:00 AM: Breakfast and morning items

9:00 AM: Gift certificates for groceries, gas, dry cleaners,
            fitness center.

Noonish: Lunch items from cooking equipment to
            restaurants

5:00 PM: Dinner items from kitchen accessories to
            restaurants

7:00 PM: Books, music, videos, etc.

This should be broke down by the hour to give each guest something specific to give. Your invitation should also reflect that. It helps to know the couple's habits and likes, which is what truly makes this theme interesting. The menu and activity can by of your choosing.

Romeo & Juliet Shower

A Time For Us....

This can be tied into the Cupid's Shower, Valentines Day Shower, or used as it is. If your guests are theater people you could take a script for everyone to read and direct your own play. You could even write your own script for that matter. When I think of this theme, it makes me want to fantasize just as I do when I'm reading a terrific romance novel....totally absorbed. The gifts here must be very romantic. It's best if you can give items that must be used as a couple.

Room Shower

Kitchen Shower
Bathroom Shower
Bedroom or Boudoir Shower
Recreation or Game Room Shower

The room shower is whatever room you choose to pick as you specific theme. Here are a few examples, then consult the section in this book on ideas and gift registry.

Season Shower

Winter, spring
summer or fall...
all you have
to do is call
you've got a friend...

The season shower is whatever season you choose to pick as your specific theme.

"Soaps" Shower

It's the Young and the Restless
in the Days of Our Lives,
Then As the World Turns
and All of Our Children's Lives
Come to this shower
as one of your soap opera's best
We'll guess your character
with lots of fun and zest.

This is the shower for the soap opera lover. This can also be the shower for all kinds of bath soaps, oils, floating candles, cosmetics, and the like. The soap opera theme shower that I attended was made interesting because the host had cut out faces of the various soap opera stars. She then had them enlarged and placed on cut tag board signs. We all put them in front of our faces and played our various roles. It was really a lot of fun.

Spice Shower

Sugar and spice, and everything nice...
That's what little girls are made of.
Frogs and snails, and puppy dog tails...
That's what little boys are made of.

Guests contribute towards a nice spice cabinet for the couple. Then each guest brings a different spice and recipe using that spice. Be sure not to duplicate. The Watkins Company in Winona, MN provides a beautiful catalogue for mail order and it is just filled with all of the spices and compatible gifts. (507) 457-3300.

Sports Shower

This is the shower just for the sport fanatics. If football, basketball, hockey, or even boxing is your thing - focus this shower around your favorite sport or team. You may even want to plan this during a game or major event, such as a championship game. Everyone should be wearing things that show off their favorite team logos.

The food should be simple. You will want to plan a menu that allows everyone to serve themselves. Some examples are: Chili, barbecues, snacks, fresh vegetables with dip, cold cuts or sandwiches, and plenty of beer on ice.

Arrange the furniture so that everyone can see the television, as well as making them comfortable for easy conversation and mingling. Plan to open gifts during half time or after the game. Give gifts that relate to their favorite team or other sporting events. This idea could also be tied into a tailgate party.

"Staples" Shower

We all know that "staples" are what we call the necessities of life. To some of us "staples" might be having food in the house. To some it might mean having plenty of beer in the refrigerator. Or maybe cigars, wine, and other liquers. Donate some canned goods to a charity in their name. Everyone has something in life that they consider very valuable for survival. Perhaps a first aid kit, fire extinguisher, smoke alarms, radon detector, and other safety items.

This is the shower where all of the guests bring a gift or "staple" as it would be. You really have to know your guests-of-honor well in order to pull this one off. Put your head together with the other guests to make your list and to avoid duplications. It could be hilarious when they open these gifts.

Surprise Shower

This shower can be any kind of theme. The purpose, of course, is to make it a surprise. If you've ever been to or were involved in a surprise gathering, you know that they are a lot of fun. The difficulty lies in the ability to keep it a surprise. That is why this type of celebration requires a tremendous amount of planning. You also have to figure out a way to pick a date for the shower with the bride and groom-to-be, but without them knowing it. Then determine how you are going to get them to the party when the time comes. Keep in mind that it isn't always easy to keep something a secret so that it is truly a SURPRISE!

Toast & Roast Shower

A requirement for this shower is that the guests should know the bride and/or groom-to-be for a fairly long time. Each guest must stand and tell humorous stories about them while presenting to them a related gift OR guests must give a sincere toast to them while presenting an appropriate gift. The guests may even select a gift first, then invent a story to go with it.

The invitations for this one should be done by telephone. First to explain the shower in more detail and to make sure the gifts are not duplicated. Secondly, to determine if the guest wishes to give a toast or a roast. You will want to have a good mix between the two.

The decorations can be simple and should include scrapbooks with pictures filled with memories that everyone can share. Hopefully, a few photos that coincide with some of the stories. The parents of the couple may even have some inspirational stories you can borrow for the event. This is a great shower to video tape as well.

Twelve Month Shower

The idea of this shower is to give the bride and groom gifts that are suitable and usable throughout the entire year. The host and hostess invite eleven of the engaged couple's friends to the party and assign each a different month from which to choose a gift. You and your co-host make the twelfth couple and also select a month for which to bring a gift.

When the gifts are presented, the couple may wish to try to guess which gift represents which month. Some suggested gifts are as follows.

January: Assorted calendars, personal diary, books to read in bad weather, crafts or hobbies, first aid supplies, outdoor thermometer, bird bath heater, electric blanket, snow shovel

February: Books are always great - maybe some relating to Washington or Lincoln in particular, foods relating to Valentine's Day like chocolate covered cherries, humidifier, air filter, "think spring" stuff....

March: Things that are green relating to spring or St. Patrick's Day, scarves for windy days, vases, ashtrays, pottery, placemats, napkins

April: Something for April showers like umbrellas or rain gear, ceramic, glass, or paper maché painted Easter eggs, pastel colored items...

May: Fresh flower arrangements or silk flower centerpieces, baskets filled with a variety of jams or scented candles, sun catchers

June: Outdoor games such as croquet, badminton, or volleyball, lap trays, patio furniture, golf accessories, items for sunny summer days

July: Tumbler or ice tea sets for outdoor use, a lawn umbrella, serving trays, fireworks or other items that are red-white-and-blue for the 4th of July

August: Books on travel, beach towels, suntan oil, picnic basket, cooler, portable cooking grill, items reminding us of the end of summer

September: College memorabilia, blankets for football games, dried flower arrangements with autumn colors, sports memorabilia

October: Gifts for Halloween like ceramic pumpkins or scary lawn ornaments, candles, outdoor wreath, fireplace matches or equipment

November: Any of the foods representative of Thanksgiving, a carving set other cutlery, a china turkey platter, painted serving bowls

December: Gifts suggesting Christmas, conversation pieces of red and green or Christmas tree ornaments, special recipes or food for the holiday season....

Wine Tasting Shower

Prosit! (German), Santa! (French), Salute! (Italian)
Skoal! (Swedish), Proose! (Dutch), Salud! (Spanish)
and CHEERS!

Or shall we say Cafe du Vin. Although a very old idea, this shower has become one of the most popular wedding showers for today's couples. This is a health-minded generation. That is why this shower allows for many creative ideas including non-alcoholic wines and beverages if preferred. It's also a perfect way to stock the couple's bar or personal wine collection. It can also be a fun way to sample and enjoy a wine tasting opportunity. Add to that the many varieties of cheese and snacks to enhance the interest of this party.

Let us begin with the couple's taste for wine. Do they have any preferences – such as red or white? Perhaps a little of both. Your local liquor store or wine shops will be happy to assist you in your selections and planning. They may even provide a wine tasting service for you that could include a party demonstration, while providing an opportunity for the guests to purchase wine as well. They often provide printed material that detail the guidelines for buying and tasting wine if you're a bit unsure.

Another suggestion is to ask each guest to bring two bottles of the same wine. One is gift wrapped with a card attached. The other is used for the wine tasting party. Guests may wish to bring an additional wine-related gift also. There are many items deemed appropriate for this occasion. From crystal wine glasses to corkscrews and winemaking kits to ice buckets or wine racks.

Some rules are as follows:

1. Serve each wine and cheese selection as a set, one at a time.

2. Rinse glasses between tasting.

3. Also serve bread, crackers, and fruit slices for variety.

4. Provide club soda and water. This is necessary to cleanse the palate, rest the taste buds, and to prevent too much alcohol.

5. It is also recommended that you provide designated drivers or arrange to pick up the guests and take them home.

Plan this shower around a cocktail hour with relaxing music. Perhaps hiring a piano player or a small jazz ensemble. Decorations can be elegant or simple. Allow a special area for the wine racks for displaying the wines and also to arrange the wineglasses. By evening's end everyone will be toasting each other.

Wish You Were Here Shower

This is the only wedding shower without the bride and groom-to-be. Friends gather together for this party and shower because the guests-of-honor live in another city that is too far away to attend. The guests bring their gifts, and share with each other what each gift is. Then, it is customary to place a telephone call to the couple during the event or afterward. A nice touch would be a speakerphone. If you're able, have everyone type an E-mail to the couple on a computer. Share some food, beverages, and fun.

Worship Shower

This shower has blossomed from the old days of ice cream socials, church bazaars, and now prayer groups. It is similar to an open-house type of shower for a church member or couple. It is generally held right after the service, but should be announced a few weeks beforehand in your church bulletin, newsletter, or a prior service. All of the families and, if your church allows, friends from outside the membership, are invited. Naturally, this one includes men and children so that the entire family can participate in the festivities.

Be sure to check with your religious advisor on any specific rules.

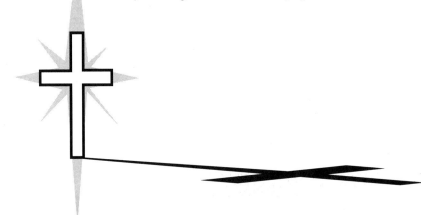

Engagement Announcement Format
Read the rules before preparing an announcement.

_____   _____
Bride-elect's Last Name   Fiance's Last Name

_____ daughter of _____
Bride-elect's Full Name   her parents

_____ _____ _____
street address   city   state

is engaged to _____ son of _____
Fiancé's Full Name   his parents

_____ _____ _____
street address   city   state

The bride-elect attends/attended/is a graduate of _____
choose appropriate phrase   educational institution

_____ _____ and is employed by
city   state

_____ _____ _____
name of employer   city   state

Her fiancé attends/attended/is a graduate of _____
choose appropriate phrase   educational institution

_____ _____ and is employed by
city   state

_____ _____ _____
name of employer   city   state

A _____ _____ wedding is planned
month   year

Engagement photograph ☐ is ☐ is not attached

Signature _____ Phone _____

_____ _____ _____
street address   city   state

Protecting your Wedding Gifts and Other Valuables

A few simple precautions will help you protect your belongings for now and for the future. Gifts you receive from friends and family will certainly have some sentimental worth, as well as cash value – so protect those valuables before, during and after the wedding.

It is suggested that you take out insurance to cover anticipated gifts. A "wedding present floater" is a special policy covering anything that won't stay in one place. The homeowners' insurance held by your parents, for instance, probably won't protect any gifts gathered in their house that you will move to your apartment. The "floater" is good for a temporary period – usually about 90 days after the wedding. It gives "blanket coverage", meaning that you don't have to list each item you're insuring, since you really don't know what the gifts will be coming in. You're protected against theft, fire, breakage, etc. There's seldom a deductible which would have you picking up part of any loss. You get back the total value.

If you already own or rent the home that you will live in, you will need regular coverage. A smarter investment, then, would be a homeowners' or renters' policy to cover all of your possessions. If you already have this type of insurance, you should "up" your coverage to include any new items you will be receiving or purchasing. For example, if your current policy is good for $7,000, you may want to "up" it an additional $2,000 to cover the gifts that you will be receiving for your wedding. Also, be sure to check with your insurance agent to see what exactly is covered.

Recording and keeping track for all your possessions and gifts may seem tedious, but it is wise to take the time to do thins. Your "Wedding Gift Register" is one of your most valuable assets. It provides you with the name and address of the gift giver, the date of acknowledgement, the item given, and the place of purchase. The "register" is your best resource for future fill-ins or replacement and evaluation for insurance purposes. When a claim is filed on a theft loss, the insurance company requires documentation of ownership. If you do not have a household inventory, receipts showing purchase are acceptable proof. However, newlyweds do not have receipts for their wedding gifts, but if you keep good documentation in your "register" you may use this for documentation of ownership.

You must also have records of all personal possessions owned by both of you before your marriage, and items purchased by you after you were married.

An inventory of everything you own, including gifts you received at showers, etc., should be taken before the wedding so that you know how much coverage you will need. All items should be recorded, indicating their cash value and age if it is a family heirloom or antique. You may wish to consult a professional appraiser for some items. Be certain your engagement ring and wedding rings have an up-to-date appraisal. The value of gold, silver, and jewels change constantly.

When taking your inventory, be sure to include clothing, sports or hobby equipment, furniture, appliances, etc. If you can find receipts for any of your items, collect them and put them in an envelope to keep on file. Also, it is a good practice to take photos of all your possessions. You should put identifying numbers on all items that can be engraved. Contact your local police department for more information on identification numbers. This practice deters thieves.

After your inventory has been taken and a list is made, you should make a copy for your records, and store the original in a safe-deposit box. Also update your records from time to time.

If all this seems unnecessary and tedious, total up the cash value of all the items on your inventory and see what an investment it represents. Does this amount surprise you? Once you realize the value of these belongings, you will probably want to take steps to assure the safety of your precious possessions! With a little thoughtful planning, the things you love can be with you for a lifetime.

Chapter 4

MENU IDEAS AND RECIPES

Peppercorn Onion Dip

1c. sour cream
1/2 c. mayonnaise
1 pkg. Good Seasons Ranch Dressing mix
2 Tbs. milk
1 tsp. ground black pepper
1/4–c. onion slices

Mix all ingredients, except onion, until well blended. Stir in onion. Chill. Serve with raw vegetables.

Hot Shrimp Dip

5 oz. Velveeta
8 oz. cream cheese
4 1/2 oz. canned shrimp
1/4 c. half and half
1/2 tsp. Worcestershire sauce
1/4 tsp. onion salt
1/8 tsp. pepper

Melt cheeses in a double boiler. Add remaining ingredients and heat thoroughly. If thinner consistency is desired, add more half–and–half. Serve warm with bread pieces or crackers.

Asparagus Appetizers

1 loaf whole wheat bread
8 oz. cream cheese
2 oz. Blue cheese
1 egg
Asparagus spears
1/2 c. melted butter

Blanch asparagus spears. Remove crust from bread slices and roll slices thin. Combine cream cheese, Blue cheese and egg. Spread on bread slices. Place one asparagus spear on each bread slice and roll up. Cut into three pieces and dip in melted butter. Freeze for later use or bake at 425 degrees on a cookie sheet for 10 to 12 minutes.

Hot Swiss and Almond Spread

1 1/2 c. (6 oz.) shredded Swiss cheese
1 (8 oz.) pkg. Philadelphia Cream Cheese, softened
1/3 c. Miracle Whip salad dressing
2 Tbs. chopped green onion
1/8 tsp. ground nutmeg
1/8 tsp. pepper
1/3 c. sliced almonds, toasted

Combine all ingredients, except almonds; mix well. Stir in almonds. Spread mixture into 9–inch pie plate. Bake at 350 degrees for 15 minutes, stirring after 8 minutes. Garnish with additional toasted almonds, if desired. Serve with assorted crackers or party rye bread slices. Makes 2 1/3 cups. Or you can spread the mixture on rye bread squares and bake 20 to 30 minutes.

Ketchup Dip

1 (7 oz.) pkg. cream cheese, softened
1/4 c. ketchup
1 Tbs. Worcestershire sauce
Small amount of milk to blend
Onion salt to taste
Garlic salt to taste
Small amount of regular salt to taste

Blend ingredients together with beater. Chill. Good with fresh vegetables.

Mini Ruebens

Party snack rye bread or crackers
8 to 12 oz. chopped corned beef
1 can Bavarian style sauerkraut, drain well
1 lb. Swiss cheese shredded
1 small bottle Thousand Island dressing

Mix together and bake at 350 degrees for 30 to 40 minutes. Spread and serve with bread or crackers.

Shrimp Dip

8 oz cream cheese
2 Tbs. sour cream
2 Tbs. French dressing 1/3 c. ketchup
1 Tbs. onion flakes
1/4 tsp. salt
1 small can shrimp drained well

Blend first six ingredients well and add shrimp.

Shrimp Dip

1 c. sour cream
2 Tbs. mayonnaise
3/4 c. coconut
1/4 c. chopped onion
1/2 c. canned mushrooms chopped
1/4 tsp. curry powder
1 can tiny drained shrimp
2 Tbs. parsley flakes
Blend ingredients well and add shrimp.

Pumpernickel Patties

1 lb. extra lean ground beef
1 lb. mild pork sausage
1 lb. pasteurized process cheese (Velveeta) and
Cut up into cubes
4 – 5 Tbs. oregano
2 loaves Pepperidge Farm cocktail rye bread slices

In skillet: Brown beef and sausage. Drain well. Add cheese. Cook on low until cheese melts. Spread on bread. Place on cookie sheet. Freeze 20 minutes. Broil 1 – 2 minutes. Serve.

Beef Spread

8 oz. cream cheese
1/2 c. sour cream
2–1/2 oz. jar dried beef, chopped
1/4 c. chopped red pepper
2 Tbs. onion flakes
1/2 tsp. or more garlic powder to taste
1/4 c. chopped pecans (optional)
2 Tbs. milk
2 Tbs. butter (optional)

Blend cream cheese, sour cream, and milk. Add beef, pepper, onion, and garlic powder. Put into 8" pie plate. Brown chopped pecans in 2 Tbs. butter and sprinkle on top. Bake at 350 degrees for 20 minutes. Serve warm on crackers or chill and serve.

Swiss Cheese–Bacon Broil

1 c. Swiss cheese, grated
1/2 c. bacon flavored bits or fry and crumble bacon
1/4 c. mayonnaise
1/4 c. ripe olives, pitted and chopped
2 Tbs. chopped green onions
Snack rye bread

Combine ingredients. Spread on snack rye bread. Place under broiler until cheese melts. Or microwave for 30 to 40 seconds.

Quick Appetizer

1 c. grated Cheddar cheese
1/4 to 1/2 c. sliced black or green olives
A little onion, chopped
Enough Miracle Whip to moisten

Mix all ingredients. Spread on Triscuit crackers. Broil until cheese melts or microwave 30 to 40 seconds.

Bacon Pinwheels

2 cans Crescent dinner rolls
1 c. sour cream
1 tsp. onion salt
1 lb. bacon, cooked and crumbled

Spread rolls out flat and spread sour cream over dough. Sprinkle onion salt over sour cram. Sprinkle bacon, roll up and slice 1/2 inch thick. Back at 350 to 375 degrees for 10 to 15 minutes or until golden brown. You can cut in half. Good to freeze and re–heat later.

Cucumber Sandwiches

1 package creme cheese
2 – 3 Cucumbers. Do not peel.

Spread creme cheese on top of cocktail size rye bread squares. Place sliced cucumber with rind on top of bread and cream cheese. Sprinkle with dill weed and serve.

Water Chestnut Wrap–A–Rounds (Simple Rumaki)

2 can water chestnuts, drained
2 lbs. semi–cooked bacon
1 Bottle or package of Teriyaki sauce, or
Worcheshire sauce and brown sugar

Wrap semi–cooked bacon around the water chestnut and put in place with a round toothpick. Place in bowl or pan with Teriyaki sauce in refrigerator for a few hours. You may want to add a dash of Worcestershire sauce and/or brown sugar to taste. Then drain off mixture and place on large cookie sheet. Place in broiler for a few minutes until bacon is cooked. Store in warming oven or small crock–pot until serving.

Taco Dip

1 jar of salsa or picante sauce.
Velveeta cheese cut up into chunks

Place ingredients in serving bowl and microwave until cheese is melted.
Serve.

Cheese and Potato Chip Sandwiches

Spread any kind of cheese spread on cocktail size rye bread squares.
Sprinkle crushed potato chips on top and serve.

Shrimp or Crab Dip

1 package soft cream cheese
1 can of pre–cooked shrimp or crab, drained
1 jar of seafood cocktail sauce.

Mix soft cream cheese and shrimp or crab together. Form into a ball and
wrap with plastic. Place in refrigerator, but remove 1 hour before serving.
Put ball on a serving platter and pour seafood cocktail sauce on top.
Arrange Ritz crackers around the dip and serve.

Steak Tartar (simple version)

1 lb. freshly ground beefsteak (Purchase the day you are going to serve it.)
1 chopped onion
Salt and pepper to taste

Mix everything together. Serve with saltine crackers. Do not use frozen ground beef. Remember to keep this fresh meat on ice or you take the risk of eating spoiled meat. This delicacy is very good eating, however you need to be careful.

Dill Pickle and Ham Wraps

1 lb. sliced lunch ham
1 jar Dill pickle spears
1 package cream cheese

Spread cream cheese on ham slices. Wrap around Dill pickle spear. Hold in place with round toothpick and serve.

Cream Cheese Balls

1 package soft cream cheese rolled into miniature balls.
1 lb. dried beef chopped very fine in a blender.

Roll the miniature cheese balls in the dried beef and serve

Celery and Cheese

1 – 2 large celery stalks, cleaned, and cut into 2 or 3" lengths.
1 package cream cheese–plain
1 package cream cheese with pineapple
1 jar cheese spread with pimentos

Fill cavity of each celery piece with a different cheese. Refrigerate and serve.

Spinach Dip

1 pint dairy sour cream (2cups)
1 c. mayonnaise
3/4 (2-3/4 oz.) pkg. dry leek soup mix, about 1/2 c.
1 (10 oz.) pkg. frozen chopped spinach, well drained
1/2 c. chopped parsley
1/2 c. chopped green onions
1 tsp. dry dill
1 tsp. dry Italian salad dressing mix
Assorted raw vegetable dippers

In a large bowl or food processor fitted with the metal blade, combine all ingredients except raw vegetables until blended. Refrigerate until ready to serve or up to 2 days. Serve dip with assorted raw vegetables. Makes 3 1/2 cups.

Liver Pâté

1/4 lb. plus 2 Tbs. butter
1/2 c. chopped onion
1 small tart apple, peeled and chopped
1 lb. chicken livers
2 to 4 Tbs. whipping cream
1/2 tsp. salt
1/4 tsp. pepper
2 whole canned pimientos, cut in very thin strips
Bread rounds or crackers

In a medium skillet over moderate heat, melt 3 tablespoons butter. Sauté onion 5 to 7 minutes until soft and lightly browned. Add apple. Cook and stir until apple is soft enough to mash with a spoon. Place onion-apple mixture into a food processor fitted with the metal blade. In the same skillet, melt 3 tablespoons of butter. Sauté livers over high heat 3 to 4 minutes, turning until they are browned on the outside and pink on the inside. Add livers to onion-apple mixture. Add 2 tablespoons cream. Process until smooth. If mixture is too thick to blend, add more cream. Place pâ té mixture in a small bowl and cool completely. Bring remaining butter to room temperature. Stir it into the cooled pâté. Add salt and pepper. Refrigerate until chilled. Place pimiento strips in a decorative manor. May be refrigerated in Crock or bowl up to 2 days.

Before serving pâté, bring to room temperature. Serve with bread rounds or assorted crackers. Makes 3 cups.

Tuna Salad

1 (12 1/2 oz.) can of tuna, drained
1 c. chopped celery
1 c. alfalfa sprouts
2 hard-cooked eggs, chopped
1/2 cup mayonnaise
1 c. shredded carrots
2/3 c. chopped green onions
1/2 c. chopped cucumber
2 tsp. lemon juice
3 Tbs. pickle relish

Place tuna in a medium bowl; flake. Mix remaining ingredients. May be refrigerated overnight. Makes 4 cups.

Marinated Stuffed Mushrooms

24 medium mushrooms
1 (12 oz.) bottle Italian salad dressing
Piquant filling:
1 (1/2 oz.) pkg. green onion dip mix
1/2 pint dairy sour cream (1 cup)
1 hard cooked egg, grated
2 Tbs. pimiento-stuffed green olives, chopped
1/4 Tbs. Tabasco sauce
Parsley sprigs

Clean mushrooms and remove stems. Place mushrooms in an 11"x17" baking dish. Pour Italian dressing over. Marinate in refrigerator several hours overnight, stirring occasionally. Prepare Piquant Filling; refrigerate.

Before serving mushrooms, spoon or pipe a small amount of filling into each mushroom cap, mounding slightly. Top each mound with a small sprig of parsley. May be refrigerated up to 5 hours. Makes 24 appetizers.

Piquant Filling:
Mix all ingredients in a small bowl until blended. May be refrigerated overnight.

Lefse Roll-ups

1-2 packages of lefse
1-2 packages of cream cheese (soft)
1-2 packages of braunsheweger

Allow lefse to sit out at room temperature for an hour prior to preparation. Lay lefse out completely flat in pie shape size. Spread on a layer of cream cheese carefully so as to not tear the lefse. Then spread a layer of braunsheweger. Roll the lefse in several rolls about 10" long. Wrap them each in aluminum foil. Refrigerate (overnight if you wish). Just prior to serving, unwrap each roll as needed and slice into 1/2" pinwheels. Serve with or without a toothpick.

Chapter 5

GIFT IDEAS AND REGISTRY

The bridal gift registry is a free service offered by department and specialty stores that gives you the opportunity to list the items you really need and want. It makes it easier for your guests to select a gift because they know that their choice is something you really want. You will also avoid getting gifts that are not compatible with your lifestyle and also avoid getting duplicates that will have to be exchanged. You should register at your favorite shops soon after you become engaged. This will be helpful to guests that will be invited to your engagement parties and showers.

Do some homework ahead of time when choosing your items for your new home. Choose these things together with your fiancé, since both of you will be sharing them. Look through magazines, newspapers, stores, etc., to decide what patterns and styles you like. Then visit your bridal gift registrar who will be able to help you with any questions you may have about coordinating all the elements that go into furnishing and accessorizing your new home.

The following is a helpful guide to use when selecting your items. Also, be sure to let your registry places know when you receive an item, so they can take it off your list to avoid duplicat ions.

Table & Other Kitchen Linen

	Size	Color	Quantity Required	Received
Tablecloths	_____	_____	_____	_____
Runners	_____	_____	_____	_____
Napkins	_____	_____	_____	_____
Napkin rings	_____	_____	_____	_____
Placemats	_____	_____	_____	_____
Dish towels	_____	_____	_____	_____
Dishcloths	_____	_____	_____	_____
Pot holders/mitts	_____	_____	_____	_____
Aprons	_____	_____	_____	_____
Appliance covers	_____	_____	_____	_____
Bathroom Linens	_____	_____	_____	_____
Bath sheets	_____	_____	_____	_____
Bath towels	_____	_____	_____	_____
Hand towels	_____	_____	_____	_____
Washcloths	_____	_____	_____	_____
Guest towels	_____	_____	_____	_____
Bath mat	_____	_____	_____	_____
Rug/lid set	_____	_____	_____	_____
Shower curtain	_____	_____	_____	_____
Scale	_____	_____	_____	_____
Hamper	_____	_____	_____	_____
Other	_____	_____	_____	_____
Bedroom Linens	_____	_____	_____	_____
Flat sheets	_____	_____	_____	_____
Fitted sheets	_____	_____	_____	_____

Pillowcases/shams	____	____	____	____
Pillows	____	____	____	____
Blankets	____	____	____	____
Bedspreads	____	____	____	____
Comforter/quilt	____	____	____	____
Mattress pads	____	____	____	____
Mattress protectors	____	____	____	____
Pillow protectors	____	____	____	____
Electric blanket	____	____	____	____

Dinnerware

Formal dinnerware is   *Casual* dinnerware is

_____   _____

by _____   by _____

Service for _____   Service for _____

Quantity			Quantity	
Required	Received		Required	Received
____	____	Dinner plates	____	____
____	____	Lunch/salad plates	____	____
____	____	Dessert plates	____	____
____	____	Bread & butter plates	____	____
____	____	Soup bowls	____	____
____	____	Cereal/fruit bowls	____	____
____	____	Tea cup & saucer	____	____
____	____	Coffee cup & saucer	____	____
____	____	Demitasse & saucer	____	____
____	____	Coffee mug	____	____

_____	_____	Covered vegetable dish	____	_____
_____	_____	Platter(s)	_____	_____
_____	_____	Salad or serving bowl	_____	_____
_____	_____	Coffee pot	_____	_____
_____	_____	Tea pot	_____	_____
_____	_____	Sugar & creamer	_____	_____
_____	_____	Gravy boat	_____	_____
_____	_____	Salt & pepper shakers	_____	_____
_____	_____	Casserole dishes	_____	_____

Notes

_____

_____

_____

_____

Serving Accessories

Formal dinnerware is   *Casual* dinnerware is

_____   _____

by _____   by _____

Service for _____   Service for _____

Quantity			Quantity	
Required	Received		Required	Received
_____	_____	Chafing dish	_____	_____
_____	_____	Compote	_____	_____
_____	_____	Coffee service	_____	_____
_____	_____	Tea service	_____	_____
_____	_____	Serving trays	_____	_____

_____	_____	Carafe	_____	_____
_____	_____	Pitchers	_____	_____
_____	_____	Serving cart	_____	_____
_____	_____	Trivets	_____	_____
_____	_____	Cake plates	_____	_____
_____	_____	Baskets	_____	_____
_____	_____	Salad bowls	_____	_____
_____	_____	Cheese board	_____	_____
_____	_____	Soup tureen	_____	_____
_____	_____	Candy dish	_____	_____
_____	_____	Platter	_____	_____
_____	_____	Candlesticks	_____	_____

Notes

_____

_____

_____

_____

Cooking Equipment & Other Kitchenware

Quantity

Required	Received		other
_____	_____	Saucepans (variety of sizes	_____
_____	_____	Skillets	_____
_____	_____	Covered casseroles (variety of sizes)	_____
_____	_____	Baking dishes (variety of sizes)	_____
_____	_____	Double boiler	_____
_____	_____	Stockpot	_____

_____	_____	Roaster & rack	_____
_____	_____	Wok	_____
_____	_____	Dutch oven	_____
_____	_____	Souffle oven	_____
_____	_____	Omelet pan	_____
_____	_____	Quiche dish	_____
_____	_____	Cookie sheets	_____
_____	_____	Muffin tins	_____
_____	_____	Bread pans	_____
_____	_____	Cake pans	_____
_____	_____	Pie pans	_____
_____	_____	Bundt pan	_____
_____	_____	Angel food cake pan	_____
_____	_____	Fondue pot	_____
_____	_____	Canister set	_____
_____	_____	Kitchen knife set	_____
_____	_____	Cutting boards	_____
_____	_____	Cookie jar	_____
_____	_____	Kitchen utensil set	_____
_____	_____	Timer	_____
_____	_____	Food scale	_____
_____	_____	Mixing bowls (variety of sizes)	_____
_____	_____	Storage containers	_____
_____	_____	Spice rack	_____
_____	_____	Egg beater	_____
_____	_____	Can/bottle opener	_____
_____	_____	Measuring cups	_____
_____	_____	Measuring spoons	_____
_____	_____	Grater	_____

_____	_____	Colander	_____
_____	_____	Ice cream scoop	_____
_____	_____	Molds	_____
_____	_____	Vegetable peeler	_____
_____	_____	Baster	_____
_____	_____	Whisks	_____
_____	_____	Thermometer	_____
_____	_____	Cheese cutter	_____
_____	_____	Cookbooks	_____

Notes

_____

_____

_____

_____

Stemware

Crystal stemware is

_____

by _____

Service for _____

Everyday stemware is

_____

by _____

Service for _____

Quantity			Quantity	
Required	Received		Required	Received
_____	_____	Water goblet	_____	_____
_____	_____	Tumbler	_____	_____
_____	_____	Fruit juice	_____	_____
_____	_____	Iced tea	_____	_____
_____	_____	Sherbet	_____	_____

_____	_____	Highball	_____	_____
_____	_____	Cocktail	_____	_____
_____	_____	Old–fashioned	_____	_____
_____	_____	Champagne	_____	_____
_____	_____	Wine	_____	_____
_____	_____	Brandy	_____	_____
_____	_____	Beer	_____	_____
_____	_____	Pitchers	_____	_____
_____	_____	Cordials	_____	_____
_____	_____	Decanters	_____	_____

Notes

_____

_____

_____

_____

Flatware

Formal flatware is

_____

by _____

Service for _____

Casual flatware is

_____

by _____

Service for _____

Quantity			Quantity	
Required	Received		Required	Received
_____	_____	Dinner knives	_____	_____
_____	_____	Steak knives	_____	_____
_____	_____	Dinner forks	_____	_____

_____	_____	Salad forks	_____	_____
_____	_____	Teaspoons	_____	_____
_____	_____	Soup spoons	_____	_____
_____	_____	Iced tea spoons	_____	_____
_____	_____	Serving spoons	_____	_____
_____	_____	Gravy ladle	_____	_____
_____	_____	Pie/cake server	_____	_____
_____	_____	Cake knife	_____	_____
_____	_____	Serving fork	_____	_____
_____	_____	Pickle fork	_____	_____
_____	_____	Cheese serving knife	_____	_____
_____	_____	Butter server	_____	_____
_____	_____	Butter spreader	_____	_____
_____	_____	Silver chest	_____	_____
_____	_____	Cutlery set	_____	_____
_____	_____	Salad serving set	_____	_____

Notes

_____

_____

_____

_____

_____

_____

_____

_____

Electric Kitchen Appliances

Quantity

Required	Received	
_____	_____	Toaster
_____	_____	Mixer
_____	_____	Blender
_____	_____	Food processor
_____	_____	Coffee maker
_____	_____	Frying pan/skillet
_____	_____	Waffle iron/griddle
_____	_____	Can opener
_____	_____	Electric knife/food slicer
_____	_____	Toaster oven
_____	_____	Warming tray
_____	_____	Slow cooker/crock pot
_____	_____	Corn popper
_____	_____	Ice cream maker
_____	_____	Pasta maker
_____	_____	Juicer
_____	_____	Steamer
_____	_____	Egg cooker
_____	_____	Wok
_____	_____	Microwave/convection oven
_____	_____	Bread maker

Notes

_____

_____

_____

Miscellaneous Items

Quantity

Required	Received		
_____	_____	Electric broom	_____
_____	_____	Vacuum cleaner	_____
_____	_____	Iron	_____
_____	_____	Ironing board	_____
_____	_____	Tool box and/or tools	_____
_____	_____	Fire extinguisher	_____
_____	_____	Smoke alarm	_____
_____	_____	Lawn equipment	_____
_____	_____	Luggage	_____
_____	_____	Sewing machine	_____
_____	_____	Barbeque equipment	_____
_____	_____	Sports equipment	_____
_____	_____	Furniture	_____
_____	_____	Area rugs	_____
_____	_____	Lamps	_____
_____	_____	Card table/chairs	_____
_____	_____	TV trays	_____
_____	_____	Decorative clocks	_____
_____	_____	Ash trays	_____
_____	_____	Candle and/or candle holders	_____
_____	_____	Vases	_____
_____	_____	Wall decorations	_____

Notes

_____

_____

Unique Items

Quantity Required	Received	Description
_____	_____	_____
_____	_____	_____
_____	_____	_____
_____	_____	_____
_____	_____	_____
_____	_____	_____
_____	_____	_____
_____	_____	_____
_____	_____	_____
_____	_____	_____
_____	_____	_____
_____	_____	_____
_____	_____	_____
_____	_____	_____
_____	_____	_____
_____	_____	_____
_____	_____	_____
_____	_____	_____
_____	_____	_____
_____	_____	_____
_____	_____	_____

Notes

_____

_____

Chapter 6

GAMES PEOPLE PLAY

Proverbial Wisdom

Fill in the blanks to complete the following "tried and true" sayings. Finish as many as you can in 5 minutes, and the person with the most correct answers wins.

1. A stich in time _____

2. Better late _____

3. Never put off until tomorrow _____

4. A watched pot _____

5. A bird in hand _____

6. What's good for the goose _____

7. There are two sides _____

8. The early bird catches _____

9. All's well _____

10. A penny saved _____

11. Absence makes _____

12. All's fair _____

13. Two can live _____

14. He who falls in love with himself _____

15. All the world _____

Gourmet Cooking

Ask each guest to unscramble each word as it relates to gourmet/cooking terminology. The person with the most correct answers wins.

1. oprliabn _____

2. chbnla _____

3. mcera _____

4. vlodssei _____

5. lgzae _____

6. treag _____

7. denak _____

8. ataemnir _____

9. hoapc _____

10. sueta _____

11. phwi _____

12. rsmmei _____

13. drhse _____

14. cnmei _____

15. kpreoco _____

Advice for being happily married Game

Place the scrambled letters on a slip of paper in a bowl and have each guest draw one. The guest that solves the most, wins.

1. A fost reswan.	A soft answer
2. Eb no mite.	Be on time
3. Evas a nepny.	Save a penny.
4. Epek glinims.	Keep smiling
5. Aveh rougeca.	Have courage.
6. Veah centipae.	Have patience
7. A miles shelp.	A smile helps.
8. Leary ot deb.	Early to bed.
9. Yeral ot sire.	Early to rise.
10. Vase nad vahe.	Save and have.
11. Gluah a tlo.	Laugh alot.
12. Od ton worth toness.	Do not throw stones.
13. Kinth phypa shoutthg.	Think happy thoughts.
14. Pleedvo sepio.	Develope poise.
15. Evol dan eb devol.	Love and be loved.
16. Kame theas owlyls.	Make haste slowly.
17. Starpice densinks.	Practice kindness.
18. Gin a gons.	Sing a song.
19. pylome item elwl.	Employ time well.
20. Sendskin spay.	Kindness pays.

Activities

Billiards	Monopoly
Bridge	Murder Mystery
Cribbage	Name That Tune
Croquet	Newlywed Game
Darts	Palm Reader
Fortune Telling	Poker
Gypsy crystal ball	Progressive Dinner
Golf	Rodeo
Hayride	Scrabble
Horseback Riding	Sherades
Horse Shoes	Taro Card Reader
Karaoke	Trivial Pursuit
Mock Trial	Volleyball
Mock Wedding	Yatzee
	Zodiac Party

Scavenger Hunt

This can be held indoors or outdoors, but requires advanced planning. If you are creative this can be a fun and challenging experience. The idea is to give everyone a list of items that they must locate. The individuals or teams that collect the most items wins.

Treasure Hunt

This game requires a lot of different clues or even a map that will eventually lead to a hidden treasure. The treasure might be gifts to the bride and groom-to-be.

Role Model in Reverse

On a piece of paper write down a variety of charachteristics that a man or woman would possess. For example:

1. A pregnant woman
2. A man changing a child's diaper
3. A woman changing a flat tire
4. A woman tieing a man's necktie

Each person acts out the choosen charachteristic and everyone tries to guess what it is and if it is a man or woman. This can be more difficult than you think, but also very funny.

Answers for Proverbial Wisdom

1. A stitch in time save nine.
2. Better late than never.
3. Never put off until tomorrow what you can do today.
4. A watched pot never boils.
5. A bird in hand is worth two in the bush.
6. What's good for the goose is good for the gander.
7. There are two sides to every question.
8. The early bird catches the worm.
9. All's well that ends well.
10. A penny saved is a penny earned.
11. Absence makes the heart grow fonder.
12. All's fair in love and war.
13. Two can live as cheaply as one.
14. He who falls in love with himself will have no rivals.
15. All the world loves a lover.

Answers for Gourmet Cooking

1. panbroil
2. blanch
3. cream
4. dissolve
5. glaze
6. grate
7. knead
8. marinate
9. poach
10. sauté
11. whip
12. simmer
13. shred
14. mince
15. precook

Chapter 7

LET'S START PLANNING

A. Talk to the guest(s)-of-honor. Discuss a date and time for the shower. Share ideas for the theme

1. Guest(s)-of-honor: _____

Address: _____

_____

Telephone: _____

2. Host/Hostess: _____

Address: _____

_____

Telephone: _____

3. Date of shower: _____

Time of shower: _____ to _____

Location of Shower: _____

_____

Address: _____

Telephone of Location: _____

Necessary paperwork, contacts, notes:_____

_____

_____

_____

4. Theme: _____

_____

_____

Special preparations and thoughts: _____

_____

_____

_____

List Vendors to call and why:

❑ A. _____

❑ B. _____

❑ C. _____

❑ D. _____

❑ E. _____

❑ F. _____

❑ G. _____

❑ H. _____

5. Invitations made or purchased _____

Guest list completed _____

Guest list addressed_____

Guest list mailed _____

R.S.V.P._____ To whom: _____

Address: _____ Telephone: _____

R.S.V.P.'s returned _____

Guests that have not R.S.V.P'd: _____

_____

_____

Where are the guest(s)-of-honor registered at:

Name of store(s): _____

_____

_____

Gift notes and ideas if needed for specific theme: _____

_____

_____

_____

6. Menu prepared

Items on menu: ❑ _____❑ _____

❑ _____❑ _____❑ _____

❑ _____❑ _____❑ _____

❑ _____❑ _____❑ _____

Ingredients to purchase: ❑ _____❑ _____

❑ _____❑ _____❑ _____

❑ _____❑ _____❑ _____

❑ _____❑ _____❑ _____

❑ _____ ❑ _____ ❑ _____

Beverages to purchase: ❑ _____ ❑ _____

❑ _____ ❑ _____ ❑ _____

❑ _____ ❑ _____ ❑ _____

❑ _____ ❑ _____ ❑ _____

❑ _____ ❑ _____ ❑ _____

7. Decorations, accessories, tableware: _____

_____

_____

Eating, serving, gift opening, game playing and other specific areas appropriate to your theme:

❑ _____

❑ _____

❑ _____

❑ _____

❑ _____

❑ _____

❑ _____

8. Special equipment:

❑ _____

❑ _____

❑ _____

❑ _____

❑ _____

❑ _____

9. Games/entertainment (if any): _____

_____

_____

_____

_____

10. Prizes (if any): _____

_____

_____

_____

_____

Notes: _____

_____

_____

_____

_____

_____

_____

_____

_____

_____

_____

THE GUEST LIST

NAME:_____

ADDRESS:_____

_____

TELEPHONE:_____

NAME:_____

ADDRESS:_____

_____

TELEPHONE:_____

NAME:_____

ADDRESS:_____

_____

TELEPHONE:_____

NAME:_____

ADDRESS:_____

_____

TELEPHONE:_____

NAME:_____

ADDRESS:_____

_____

TELEPHONE:_____

NAME:_____

ADDRESS:_____

_____

TELEPHONE:_____

NAME:_____

ADDRESS:_____

_____

TELEPHONE:_____

NAME:_____

ADDRESS:_____

_____

TELEPHONE:_____

NAME:_____

ADDRESS:_____

_____

TELEPHONE:_____

NAME:_____

ADDRESS:_____

_____

TELEPHONE:_____

NAME:_____

ADDRESS:_____

_____

TELEPHONE:_____

NAME:_____

ADDRESS:_____

_____

TELEPHONE:_____

NAME:_____

ADDRESS:_____

_____

TELEPHONE:_____

NAME:_____

ADDRESS:_____

_____

TELEPHONE:_____

NAME:_____

ADDRESS:_____

_____

TELEPHONE:_____

NAME:_____

ADDRESS:_____

_____

TELEPHONE:_____

NAME:_____

ADDRESS:_____

_____

TELEPHONE:_____

NAME:_____

ADDRESS:_____

_____

TELEPHONE:_____

NAME:_____

ADDRESS:_____

_____

TELEPHONE:_____

NAME:_____

ADDRESS:_____

_____

TELEPHONE:_____

NAME:_____

ADDRESS:_____

_____

TELEPHONE:_____

NAME:_____

ADDRESS:_____

_____

TELEPHONE:_____

NAME:_____

ADDRESS:_____

_____

TELEPHONE:_____

NAME:_____

ADDRESS:_____

_____

TELEPHONE:_____

NAME:_____

ADDRESS:_____

_____

TELEPHONE:_____

NAME:_____

ADDRESS:_____

_____

TELEPHONE:_____

NAME:_____

ADDRESS:_____

_____

TELEPHONE:_____

NAME:_____

ADDRESS:_____

_____

TELEPHONE:_____

NAME:_____

ADDRESS:_____

_____

TELEPHONE:_____

NAME:_____

ADDRESS:_____

_____

TELEPHONE:_____

Chapter 8

SHOWERS FOR OTHER OCCASIONS

Divorce Shower

This is a shower when a surprise can really be fun. If you have a friend that is down–in–the–dumps and, perhaps, came out badly in a divorce emotionally or financially, this is a perfect way to bring their spirits up. Likewise, if you have a friend that is very happy about their divorce, why not celebrate his or her new future.

The gifts for this shower depend upon what your friend wants or needs. Sometimes a person needs really basic things like dishes or pots and pans. In other cases, the gifts can possibly be just for fun.

Singles Shower

You don't have to be engaged to have a party and receive a gift that you might need. Schedule a party with your friends to exchange names and treat each other to something nice for your home or apartment. You could even plan a series of parties, each of your friends hosting for one another.

Serve wedding reception foods as a mockery to getting married. Provide beverages and share in lots of girl talk...or guy talk.

Baby Shower (adoption also)

Many of themes in this book will work for an expecting mother. The obvious, however, is that the gifts are for the future newborn.

No one seems to know just where or when baby showers began. Bridal showers were popular in the United States as early as 1900, but baby showers as we know them today did not become commonplace until shortly after World War II – possibly the first manifestation of the baby boom. Prior to that time, gift giving to new parents was usually more of an informal event – a hand made gift for baby's layette, given after the baby was born.

Baby showers have always filled several basic needs. They help the new parents acquire things a baby needs, which might otherwise drain the family budget. Baby showers also provide emotional support for an expectant couple who may be facing some anxiety about their new roles. And baby showers are ideal for celebrating the birth of a child – marking the passage of an important stage of life. Finally, they can be just plain fun!

Remember: Baby showers aren't just for first–time parents. Every baby deserves a special welcome by parents' family, friends and co–workers . As a matter of fact, the more children already in a family, the more the expectant parents will enjoy a baby shower; updating the requisite supply of baby necessities is always practical. Just as important is the sharing of joy every baby adds to a family.

By the way – do consider inviting men. Just work a little harder to dispel their stereotypes of showers for women only.

Anniversary Shower

This shower is based on the old fashioned idea of gift giving. See the anniversary list below, you can follow the traditional method of a gift that is symbolic for that year – or ask each guest to bring a gift for each different year of the marriage. Show old photographs – especially wedding.

Remembering the Anniversaries

First	Paper
Second	Cotton
Third	Leather
Fourth	Books
Fifth	Wood
Sixth	Iron
Seventh	Copper
Eighth	Electric
Ninth	Pottery
Tenth	Tin
Eleventh	Steel
Twelfth	Linen
Thirteenth	Lace
Fourteenth	Ivory
Fifteenth	Crystal
Twentieth	China
Twenty–fifth	Silver
Thirtieth	Pearl
Thirty–fifth	Coral
Fortieth	Ruby
Forty–fifth	Sapphire
Fiftieth	Gold
Fifty–fifth	Emerald
Sixtieth	Diamond

"Stag" or "Stagette" Shower

This is it girls – the counterpart to the infamous stag party. Let your imagination go to work. Hire a male/female stripper or dancer. Take some polaroid pictures of this one. You'll be laughing for a long time.

Off to College
1st Apartment
Entering the Service
Welcome Home
Moving Away
New Neighbors
Home Decorating
Graduation

SAMPLE
INVITATION

Bridal Shower

FOR:

DATE:

TIME:

PLACE:

THEME:

WEDDING REGISTRY AT:

GIVEN BY:

R.S.V.P.